IELTS
PRACTICE TESTS

· PETER MAY ·

with explanatory key

OXFORD
UNIVERSITY PRESS

OXFORD
UNIVERSITY PRESS

Great Clarendon Street, Oxford OX2 6DP

Oxford University Press is a department of the University of Oxford.
It furthers the University's objective of excellence in research, scholarship,
and education by publishing worldwide in

Oxford New York

Auckland Bangkok Buenos Aires Cape Town Chennai
Dar es Salaam Delhi Hong Kong Istanbul Karachi Kolkata
Kuala Lumpur Madrid Melbourne Mexico City Mumbai
Nairobi São Paulo Shanghai Taipei Tokyo Toronto

OXFORD and OXFORD ENGLISH are registered trade marks of
Oxford University Press in the UK and in certain other countries

Acknowledgements

The authors and publisher are grateful to those who have given
permission to reproduce the following extracts and adaptations
of copyright material:

pp23-24 'Vanished' by Douglas McInnis published by *New Scientist*,
6 December 2003. Reproduced by permission of *New Scientist*.

pp28-29 'Dogs: a Love Story' by Angus Phillips, *National Geographic*,
January 2002. Reprinted by permission of *National Geographic*.

p32 'Selected countries of residence of visitor arrivals' from Australian
Social Trends 2002 Education - Participation in Education: Overseas
students

pp44-45 'Combating loneliness and homesickness', from
www.nusonline.co.uk/content/advice. Reproduced by permission of
National Union of Student.

pp46-47 'Oxford University Language Centre Library FAQs', from
www.lang.ox.co.uk. Reproduced by permission of Oxford University
Language Centre.

pp50-51 'Scratching the surface' by David Hambling, *The Guardian*,
28 November 2002. Reproduced by permission of David Hambling.

pp59-60 'Life, but not as we know it' by Henry Gee, *The Guardian*,
22 February 2001. Reproduced by permission of Henry Gee.

p75 'Students with disabilities'. Reproduced with the permission of
Nelson Thornes Ltd from *Push Guide to Choosing a New University* 2nd
Edition (2004) - ISBN 07487 90276.

pp78-79 'How fireworks work' by Marshall Brain from
www.science.howstuffworks.com/fireworks. Reproduced by permission
of *howstuffworks*.

pp80-81 'Unmasking skin' by Joel L Swerdlow, *National Geographic*,
November 2002. Reprinted by permission of *National Geographic*.

pp85-86 'How Lock Picking Works' by Tom Harris and Marshall Brain
from www.science.howstuffworks.com/lockpicking. Reproduced by
permission of *howstuffworks*.

pp88-89 'Stars without the stripes' by Richard Scase, *The Observer*, 1 July
2001. Reproduced by permission of Richard Scase.

p102 'The Secret Strike' by Tim Thwaites published by *New Scientist*,
6 December 2003. Reproduced by permission of *New Scientist*.

pp103-104 'The Power of Light' by Joel Achenbach, *National Geographic*,
October 2001. Reprinted by permission of *National Geographic*.

pp112-113 'The Ring Cycle' by Mike Baillie, *The Guardian*: Frontiers 01,
Science and Technology 2001-2002, ed. T Radford, Atlantic Books 2002.
Reproduced by permission of Mike Baillie.

p115 'Teenagers aged 13-19 years and the total population:
hospitalisation rates for certain' from Australian Social Trends 2002
Family Living Arrangements: Selected risks faced by teenagers. ABS data
used with permission from the Australian Bureau of Statistics
www.abs.gov.au.

Sources

p92 www.un.org/millenniumgoals/

Although every effort has been made to trace and contact copyright
holders before publication, this has not been possible in some cases.
We apologize for any apparent infringement of copyright and if notified,
the publisher will be pleased to rectify any errors or omissions at the
earliest opportunity.

The publisher is grateful to the University of Cambridge Local
Examinations Syndicate for permission to reproduce IELTS
answer sheets.

The publisher would like to thank the following for their permission to
reproduce photographs.

Alamy Images pp80 (cactus thorn and finger/Gerard Maas), 81 (water
poured on hand/Pixland); Corbis pp28 (wolf pack/Tom Brakefield),
55 (canal boat/Buddy Mays); Frank Lane Picture Agency pp28 (sheep and
dogs/Foto Natura Catalogue), 112 (tree rings/Maurice Nimmo); Image100
p88(presentation); Kobal Collection p59 (Day the Earth); OUP pp19
(astronaut over Earth/PhotoDisc), 103 (lightning/PhotoDisc),
103 (eclipse/PhotoDisc).

Illustrations by

Julian Baker pp49, 57, 78, 86

Mark Duffin pp23, 64, 79, 99, 107

Nigel Paige pp50

Contents

Introduction

This book contains four complete practice tests for IELTS (the International English Language Testing System), covering the Listening, Academic Reading, Academic Writing and Speaking modules in each test. It is intended for use either as part of a classroom preparation course for the exam or for self-study at home.

Test 1 and Test 2 contain extensive advice and thorough training for all the most common question types used in the exam. The explanatory key edition also contains explanations for why answers are correct. It is recommended that self-study students use the explanatory key edition.

How to use this book

Begin by reading this Introduction, referring to each component of the book in turn. Then read the helpful advice on each module in the IELTS Factfile on pages 6–9.

The next step is to work through Tests 1 and 2. To get the most from the training they contain, follow this special procedure:

- Before beginning each exam task, read the *Strategies* which describe how to approach it.
- Then answer the questions in *Improve your skills*. Remember to check your answers to these, which are located at the end of each test.
- Finally, attempt the exam task, making use of the skills you have learned.

In Tests 3 and 4, you can apply the skills you have developed. Any of the tests can also be done under exam conditions, including Tests 1 and 2, provided you leave the *Strategies* and *Improve your skills* until after you finish.

If using the explanatory key edition, you can also check your answers and review questions which you found difficult.

Exam training

Strategies

Tests 1 and 2 cover the most common IELTS task types and their main variations. The *Strategies* give a series of clear instructions on how to approach each task type, from analysing the question to expressing your answers.

For each Writing task in Tests 1–3, these are divided into *Question* and *Composition Strategies*:

Question Strategies show you how to interpret the question and plan your essay. For Writing Task 1 you also learn how to process visual information quickly, while for Writing Task 2 you find out how to choose your approach to the topic.

Composition Strategies focus on how to write your essay, including content, organization, appropriate language, linking devices, and style.

Improve your skills

For each task in Tests 1 and 2, there is also at least one *Improve your skills* feature. These put the *Strategies* into practice, helping you develop the skills you need to tackle exam questions. For example, the exercise may check your understanding of the instructions or may ask you to predict answers before you listen or read.

Before you go on to the exam task, you should check your answers in the *Improve your skills* key at the end of each Test.

Explanatory key

You can use the explanatory key to confirm or find out why particular answers are correct. In the case of multiple-choice, matching lists, and other question types in which there are several options, it also explains why some are incorrect.

For the Listening module, the notes may also draw your attention to the 'prompt': the word or phrase you hear which tells you that the answer to a particular question is coming soon. The relevant extract from the script occurs immediately after the explanations for each set of questions. Words, phrases or sentences relating to each answer are in bold in the script.

Sample writing answers

This section contains sample answers to all tasks in the writing modules. These are written by students, so it should be remembered that there are always different ways of approaching each one. All the sample answers are accompanied by comments made by an experienced IELTS Examiner. These comments are a useful guide to the main strengths and weaknesses of each essay. You may find it helpful to look for examples of positive and negative points in these and to think about them when you are planning and writing similar essays of your own.

The tests

The four tests within this book are at IELTS exam level. They contain a range of topics that are representative of the IELTS examination. Topics for Reading and Writing have been chosen to reflect the Academic modules for those skills.

Tests 1 and 2 are focused on exam training, but all four tests can also be used under exam conditions.

You will require:

- a quiet place to work, free from interruptions
- writing materials
- a CD-player
- a clock or watch to ensure you keep to the time allowed

For the Listening module, play it through to the end, without a pause, and write your answers. When the recording ends, stop writing and don't listen again to any part of it. The listening modules for Tests 3 and 4 have been recorded to be used in this way. For the other modules, keep strictly to the time indicated.

The IELTS examination

The academic version of the IELTS examination assesses whether you are ready to begin a university course in English. It is widely recognized for courses in countries around the world.

Taking the exam

There are IELTS tests centres in over 105 countries, where it can be taken on a number of possible dates each year. Candidates should have a good level of English and be aged at least 16. It is advisable to find out well in advance what score is needed to enter a university or other institution.

Candidates take the Listening, Reading and Writing modules all on one day, with the Speaking module either on the same day or within a week of these three. Two weeks later, each candidate receives a Test Report Form. This shows their score for each module on a scale from 1 to 9, as well as an average over the four modules.

As with all other exams of this kind, the test score is valid for two years. Candidates can repeat the exam after three months, although each time you take IELTS you have to sit all four modules.

Special facilities and provisions are available for disabled candidates, for example if they suffer from visual or hearing difficulties, or if they have a specific learning difficulty.

For further information on all aspects of the exam, see the IELTS Handbook or contact Cambridge ESOL, the British Council, or IDP Education Australia.

IELTS Factfile

The exam is divided into four modules, taken in the following order.

Listening
30 minutes

In each section you will hear a recording. The four sections become progressively more difficult and each recording is played once only. There are pauses to divide the recording into smaller parts. For each part you need to answer a series of questions of one type.

Section	Number of items	Text type	Task types
1	10	social or transactional conversation (2 speakers)	completing notes, table, sentences, diagram, flow chart or summary
2	10	talk or speech on social needs (1 speaker)	short-answer questions
3	10	conversation in educational context (2–4 speakers)	various kinds of multiple-choice questions
4	10	talk or lecture on topic of general interest (1 speaker)	labelling parts of a diagram
			classification
			matching lists
			sentence completion
			correcting notes

Tips and hints

- Read the questions before each section of the recording begins.
- Use the pauses to prepare for the next set of questions.
- Study the instructions to find out what you have to write and where.
- Use the example at the beginning of the first section to familiarize yourself with the sound, the situation, and the speakers.
- Keep listening all the time, looking only at the questions that relate to the part being played.
- Remember that the topics are non-technical and no more difficult for you than for students of other subjects.
- Answer questions in the order they appear on the Question Paper – they normally follow the order of information in the recording.
- You have some time after the tape ends to transfer your answers to the Answer Sheet – check your grammar and spelling as you do so.
- There may be a variety of English accents and dialects, so practise listening to speakers from different places and backgrounds.

Academic Reading

60 minutes

The three passages contain 2000–2750 words in total and become progressively more difficult, but they are always suitable for non-specialist readers. If any technical terms are used, they will be explained in a glossary. While the number of questions for each passage may vary, there are always forty items in total.

Passage	Number of items	Text type	Task types
1	11–15	topics of general interest	various kinds of multiple-choice questions
			short-answer questions
2	11–15	non-specialist articles or extracts from books, journals, magazines and newspapers	sentence completion
			classification
3	11–15		matching headings with paragraphs or sections of text
			completing notes, sentences, tables, summary, diagram or flow chart
		one, at least, has detailed logical argument	matching lists/phrases
			matching information with paragraphs
			true/false/not given (text information)
			yes/no/not given (writer's views)

Tips and hints

- First read each passage quickly and ask yourself questions, e.g. What is the topic? Where is the text probably taken from? What is the writer's main purpose? Who is the intended reader? In what style is it written?
- Don't try to understand the exact meaning of every word. There isn't time, and a particular word or sentence may not be tested anyway.
- Study any example answer and decide why it is correct.
- If you have to choose from alternatives, check how many of them you have to use.
- Check whether you have to use words from the text in your answers or your own words.
- Keep to the stated word limit by avoiding unnecessary words in your answer.
- If a question type uses both unfinished statements and direct questions, decide which are which and check the grammar of your answers.
- After you fill in all the answers on a diagram, chart or table, check that it makes sense overall.

Academic Writing
60 minutes

There is no choice of task, either in Part 1 or 2, so you must be prepared to write about any topic. However, the topics in the exam are of general interest and you do not need to be an expert to write about them.

Task	Time	Format	Task types
1	20 minutes	150-word report, describing or explaining a table or diagram	presenting information based on: • data, e.g. bar charts, line graph, table • a process/procedure in various stages • an object, event or series of events
2	40 minutes	250-word essay, responding to a written opinion/problem	presenting and/or discussing: • your opinions • solutions to problems • evidence, opinions and implications • ideas or arguments

Tips and hints

- Your answer must be relevant to the task: never write pre-prepared sections of text.
- There are no marks for copying the question in your answer, but if you wish you can rephrase it in your own words.
- There is a minimum number of words, but no maximum. This means that if you write fewer than 150 words you will lose marks.
- Task 2 carries more marks than Task 1, so keep to the suggested timing.
- Always leave some time to check your essay after you have finished.
- Essays are often on topics that are of current interest: read and listen to the news on a wide range of subjects, thinking about the issues involved.

In Task 1, you are tested on:

Task Fulfilment – answer the question, keeping to the topic at all times.

Coherence and Cohesion – organize your writing well, connecting your ideas and sentences with suitable linking expressions.

Vocabulary and Sentence Structure – use a wide range of language both accurately and appropriately.

In Task 2, you are tested on:

Arguments, Ideas and Evidence – show you can discuss these and put forward your own opinions.

Communicative Quality – express your ideas clearly, organizing and linking them logically.

Vocabulary and Sentence Structure – use a wide range of language both accurately and appropriately.

Speaking
11–14 minutes

You will be interviewed, on your own, by one Examiner, and the conversation will be recorded on audio cassette. The three-part structure of the interview is always the same, although the topics will vary from candidate to candidate.

Part	Time	Format	Task types
1	4–5 minutes	introduction, interview	• Introduction, ID check • You answer questions about yourself, your home/family, job/studies, interests, other familiar topics.
2	3–4 minutes	independent long turn	• You are given a topic verbally and on a card. You have a minute to prepare a talk. • You speak for 1–2 minutes on the topic, e.g. a person, place, object or event. • You answer one or two follow-up questions.
3	4–5 minutes	two-way discussion	• You answer verbal questions, discussing more abstract ideas linked to the topic of Part 2.

Tips and hints

- Do not try to make any kind of prepared speech.
- Add to any 'Yes' or 'No' answers you give, explaining at least one point.
- Remember that it is your ability to communicate effectively that is being assessed, not your general knowledge.
- Speak directly to the Examiner, not to the cassette player.
- The Examiner cannot tell you the result of this (or any other) module: don't ask for comments.
- Practise for Part 2 by speaking continuously for 1–2 minutes, timing yourself with a clock or watch.

In all parts of Speaking, you are tested on the following:

Fluency and Coherence – talk at normal speed, without over-long pauses. Organize your ideas and sentences logically, connecting them with suitable linking expressions.

Lexical Resource – use a wide range of vocabulary both precisely and appropriately to express your ideas.

Grammatical Range and Accuracy – use a wide range of structures. Try to make as few errors as possible, in particular avoid any that make it difficult to understand you.

Pronunciation – make sure that your speech sounds natural and that it can be understood at all times.

Test 1

Listening 30 minutes

Section 1

Questions 1–7

Improve your skills: focusing on speakers

Study the instructions, heading, notes, and example for 1–7.
Answer questions a–d.

a Who do you think will be speaking to whom? Why?
b Where do you think the speakers are?
c Do you think their tone will be formal or conversational?
d What kind of information will you have to write?

► Check your answers on page 39 before you continue.

Complete the notes below.
Write NO MORE THAN THREE WORDS AND/OR A NUMBER for
each answer.

Check your answers on page 39 before you continue.

**Strategies:
completing notes**

Before you listen, think
about who the speakers
are likely to be, where
they are, and why they are
speaking.

Listen to the example to
check your predictions
about the speakers.

Listen for the words or
numbers that you need.
Write what you hear or a
good short alternative.

Write numbers as figures,
not as words, e.g. *19*, not
nineteen.

After you listen, check that
your completed notes
make sense.

Check your spelling – you
may lose marks for
mistakes.

Notes – Clark's Bicycle Hire

Example   Answer

Type: ... *touring* ... bike

Rental: £50 a week, or 1 £ .... a day

Late return fee: 2 £ .... per extra hour

Deposit: 3 £ .... returnable

Accessories: £5 for 4 .... : pannier or handlebar type

free: pump

        repair kit

        5 strong ....

Insurance: included, but must pay first 6 £ .... of claim

Pay: by 7 .... only

Study the main features
of the map and notice
how they are connected,
e.g. by roads, footpaths
or corridors.

Decide what the possible
answers have in common,
e.g. they are all rooms,
buildings or streets.

Listen for the names of all
the places you are given
and for prepositions of
place, e.g. *near to*,
in front of.

Questions 8–10

Improve your skills: understanding the task

Study the instructions and map for 8–10. Then answer these questions.

a Do you have to write letters, names from a list, or your own answers?
b How many names do you have to write in?
c Which names are already given on the map?

▶ Check your answers on page 39 before you continue.

Improve your skills: identifying main features

Familiarize yourself with the map, then ask yourself these questions.

a Which building is next to the park?
b Where is 8 in relation to the police station?
c Where is the pharmacy in relation to 9?
d What is behind the pharmacy?

▶ Check your answers on page 39 before you continue.

Label the map. Choose your answers from the box below.

Write the appropriate letters A–E on the map.

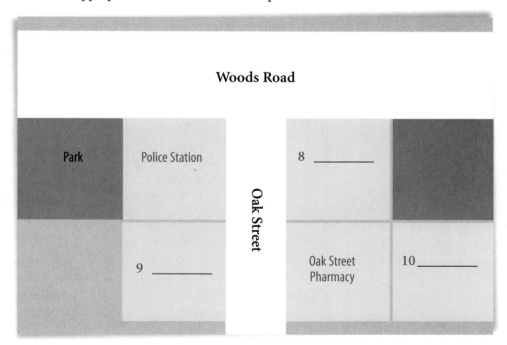

A   health centre
B   Maple Leaf pub
C   Clark's Cycle Hire
D   supermarket
E   garage

Section 2

Questions 11–17

Improve your skills: predicting from examples

Look at the table below. *Rugby* and *tennis* are given as examples of sports. What answers would you predict for spaces 12, 14 and 15 from the examples given?

▶ Check your answers on page 39 before you continue

Complete the table below.

Write NO MORE THAN THREE WORDS for each answer.

Before you listen, check
how many words you can
use and decide what kind
you need to write, e.g.
nouns, verbs.

Study the headings and
examples, which will
indicate the kind of
information required. Try
to guess some of the
missing words.

While you hear the
recording, use the
information in the table to
guide you through the
questions.

Write in your answers as
you listen, checking
whether your guesses are
confirmed or not.

Don't expect to write any
information on shaded
parts of the table.

TYPE OF CLUB OR SOCIETY	EXAMPLES
SPORTS	rugby tennis
HOBBY/INTEREST	landscape photography 11 ....
12	dancing speed-dating
RELIGIOUS	
INTERNATIONAL/CULTURAL	13 .... Afro-Caribbean
14	human rights environmental
15	Republicans 16 ....
PERFORMING ARTS	17 .... amateur theatre

Questions 18–20

Improve your skills: predicting from stems

Look at Questions 18–20. What is the stem of each one? What do you think will be discussed in relation to each?

▶ Check your answers on page 39 before you continue

Choose the correct letters A–C.

18 In this city, clubs and societies are mainly paid for by

    A   embassies of other countries.

    B   individual members.

    C   the city council.

19 Finding the right club might influence your choice of

    A   city.

    B   district.

    C   friends.

20 What should you do if the right club does not exist?

    A   set one up yourself

    B   find one on the Internet

    C   join one in another town

Section 3

Strategies: completing a flow-chart

Before you listen, study the language used in the chart and decide what its purpose is, e.g. to ask questions, to state facts. This may give you clues to the type of answers needed.

Identify the style of the language used, e.g. note-form, and write your answer in the same style.

While you listen, remember that the arrows show you how the text is organized.

After you have listened, check that the completed flow chart reflects the overall sense of the recording.

Questions 21–25

Improve your skills: looking for clues

Study the language used in the flow chart and answer these questions.

a Which verb form is used in the sentences? What does this tell you about the purpose of these sentences?

b In what style are the sentences written? Which kinds of words, therefore, can you leave out of your answers?

▶ Check your answers on page 39 before you continue.

Label the flow chart. Write NO MORE THAN THREE WORDS for each answer.

LECTURES AND NOTE TAKING

Complete all 21 .... before lecture

⬇

Think about likely 22 .... of lecture.

⬇

Take notes during lecture.

⬇

23 .... immediately after lecture.

↙ ↘

Revise before 24 ....   Revise every 25 ....

Questions 26–29

Improve your skills: identifying key words

Underline the key words in each of 26–29, e.g. question 26 *where, sit, attend*.

▶ Check your answers on page 39 before you continue

Improve your skills: question forms

Which of answers 26–29 requires you to listen for:

a a reason?
b a type of word or phrase?
c a place?
d an action?

▶ Check your answers on page 39 before you continue.

Write NO MORE THAN THREE WORDS for each answer.

26 Where should you sit when you attend a lecture? ....

27 What should you do if you miss an important point? ....

28 Why must your notes be easy to read? ....

29 What do we call expressions which indicate what is coming next? ....

Question 30

Improve your skills: describing diagrams

Study question 30 and diagrams A–D. Then answer these questions.

a What are the words for everything you can see in the diagrams?
b In what ways are A–D similar? How do they differ?
c What other expressions like those in (a) above do you know?

▶ Check your answers on page 39 before you continue

Circle the correct letter A, B, C or D.

30 Where does Carlos write summing-up points on his notes?

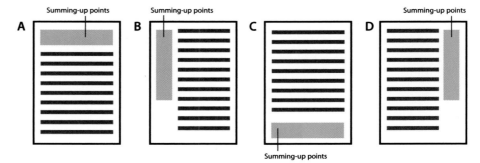

Section 4

Strategies:
completing a summary

Before you listen, quickly read the text to understand the main points.

Look at the context of each question, thinking about the type of expression you may need to use, e.g. a city, a month.

As you listen, don't get stuck on any difficult questions: you may miss the answers to the next ones.

When the recording has ended, check the summary makes sense overall and that your answers fit both logically and grammatically. Also check you have spelt words correctly and written any numbers clearly.

Improve your skills: understanding the overall meaning

Answer these questions about the summary text before you listen.

a   In which country is Coober Pedy?
b   What is its main industry?
c   When did the boom happen? Why?
d   Where do some people live? Why? What else is there?

▶   Check your answers on page 39 before you continue

Improve your skills: what kind of word?

What type of word is probably needed for each of 31–36? Choose from these (there are two you don't need to use):

a percentage   a year   a number   a person
an historical event   a building   an object   a part of the world

▶   Check your answers on page 39 before you continue

Complete the summary below by writing NO MORE THAN THREE WORDS in the spaces provided.

The Australian mining town of Coober Pedy is about 31 ....

kilometres south of Alice Springs. Opals were first found in the area in

32 .... and people began to settle there after the

33 .... In the late 1940s, new opal fields and mass immigration

from 34 .... created a boom, despite the extreme climate which

forced about 35 .... of the population to live underground,

where they built hotels, churches, and the world's only underground

36 ....

Strategies: matching lists

Before you listen, study the task. If there are more questions than options, you will need to use one or more options at least once. Sometimes, a particular option may not be needed at all.

For each list, identify the key words and try to think of synonyms for them.

Listen for the key words in the questions and for expressions with similar meanings to those in the options.

Write only the letters as your answers.

If you really can't decide on an answer: guess. You don't lose marks for being wrong, so answer every question.

Improve your skills: thinking of synonyms

1 Study the options. The key word in option A is *in*. What are the key words in B and C?
2 Note down words and phrases with similar meanings to the key words in A, B and C, e.g. in: *within*, *inside*

▶ Check your answers on page 39 before you continue

*Write the appropriate letters **A**, **B**, or **C** against Questions 37–40.*

What are the locations of the following places?

Example	*Answer*
the conical hills	**B**
37 the town of Woomera	………
38 the opal museum	………
39 the Dingo Fence	………
40 the sets of films	………

A	in the town of Coober Pedy
B	near Coober Pedy
C	far from Coober Pedy

Academic Reading 1 hour

Reading Passage 1

*You should spend about 20 minutes on **Questions 1–14**, which are based on Reading Passage 1.*

Check your answers on page 40 before you continue.

Check your answers on page 40 before you continue.

Strategies: matching headings to paragraphs

Look at the list of headings.

Read quickly through the text, highlighting the key sentence in each paragraph and summarizing the main ideas in your mind. Don't try to understand every word.

Study the examples and cross them off the list of headings.

Match the main idea of each paragraph with a heading. Lightly cross out headings as you choose them.

When you finish, check that no remaining headings fit anywhere.

Questions 1–5

Improve your skills: identifying key sentences

Find the key sentence in each paragraph, e.g. paragraph A: 1st sentence.

▶ Check your answers on page 40 before you continue.

Improve your skills: focusing on examples

Study the example answers given below. Why is iv the correct heading for paragraph A? Why is ii the correct heading for paragraph F?

▶ Check your answers on page 40 before you continue.

*Reading Passage 1 has seven paragraphs **A–G**.*

*Choose the correct heading for paragraphs **B–E** and **G** from the list of headings below. Write the correct number (**i–x**) in boxes 1–5 on your answer sheet.*

List of Headings
i   The problem of dealing with emergencies in space
ii   How space biomedicine can help patients on Earth
iii   Why accidents are so common in outer space
iv   What is space biomedicine?
v   The psychological problems of astronauts
vi   Conducting space biomedical research on Earth
vii   The internal damage caused to the human body by space travel
viii How space biomedicine first began
ix   The visible effects of space travel on the human body
x   Why space biomedicine is now necessary

Example	Paragraph **A**	*Answer*	iv

1   Paragraph **B**
2   Paragraph **C**
3   Paragraph **D**
4   Paragraph **E**

Example	Paragraph **F**	*Answer*	ii

5   Paragraph **G**

Space travel AND health

A Space biomedicine is a relatively new area of research both in the USA and in Europe. Its main objectives are to study the effects of space travel on the human body, identifying the most critical medical problems and finding solutions to those problems. Space biomedicine centres are receiving increasing direct support from NASA and/or the European Space Agency (ESA).

B This involvement of NASA and the ESA reflects growing concern that the feasibility of travel to other planets, and beyond, is no longer limited by engineering constraints but by what the human body can actually withstand. The discovery of ice on Mars, for instance, means that there is now no necessity to design and develop a spacecraft large and powerful enough to transport the vast amounts of water needed to sustain the crew throughout journeys that may last many years. Without the necessary protection and medical treatment, however, their bodies would be devastated by the unremittingly hostile environment of space.

C The most obvious physical changes undergone by people in zero gravity are essentially harmless; in some cases they are even amusing. The blood and other fluids are no longer dragged down towards the feet by the gravity of Earth, so they accumulate higher up in the body, creating what is sometimes called 'fat face', together with the contrasting 'chicken legs' syndrome as the lower limbs become thinner.

D Much more serious are the unseen consequences after months or years in space. With no gravity, there is less need for a sturdy skeleton to support the body, with the result that the bones weaken, releasing calcium into the bloodstream. This extra calcium can overload the kidneys, leading ultimately to renal failure. Muscles too lose strength through lack of use. The heart becomes smaller, losing the power to pump oxygenated blood to all parts of the body, while the lungs lose the capacity to breathe fully. The digestive system becomes less efficient, a weakened immune system is increasingly unable to prevent diseases and the high levels of solar and cosmic radiation can cause various forms of cancer.

E To make matters worse, a wide range of medical difficulties can arise in the case of an accident or serious illness when the patient is millions of kilometres from Earth. There is simply not enough room available inside a space vehicle to include all the equipment from a hospital's casualty unit, some of which would not work properly in space anyway. Even basic things such as a drip depend on gravity to function, while standard resuscitation techniques become ineffective if sufficient weight cannot be applied. The only solution seems to be to create extremely small medical tools and 'smart' devices that can, for example, diagnose and treat internal injuries using ultrasound. The cost of designing and producing this kind of equipment is bound to be, well, astronomical.

F Such considerations have led some to question the ethics of investing huge sums of money to help a handful of people who, after all, are willingly risking their own health in outer space, when so much needs to be done a lot closer to home. It is now clear, however, that every problem of space travel has a parallel problem on Earth that will benefit from the knowledge gained and the skills developed from space biomedical research. For instance, the very difficulty of treating astronauts in space has led to rapid progress in the field of telemedicine, which in turn has brought about developments that enable surgeons to communicate with patients in inaccessible parts of the world. To take another example, systems invented to sterilize waste water on board spacecraft could be used by emergency teams to filter contaminated water at the scene of natural disasters such as floods and earthquakes. In the same way, miniature monitoring equipment, developed to save weight in space capsules, will eventually become tiny monitors that patients on Earth can wear without discomfort wherever they go.

G Nevertheless, there is still one major obstacle to carrying out studies into the effects of space travel: how to do so without going to the enormous expense of actually working in space. To simulate conditions in zero gravity, one tried and tested method is to work under water, but the space biomedicine centres are also looking at other ideas. In one experiment, researchers study the weakening of bones that results from prolonged inactivity. This would involve volunteers staying in bed for three months, but the centre concerned is confident there should be no great difficulty in finding people willing to spend twelve weeks lying down. All in the name of science, of course.

These focus on particular points. For each question, highlight the key words.

Go back to the part of the text where you remember this point being mentioned.

Read through that part for the key words, or words with similar meaning, and highlight them.

Read the question again and decide on your answer, taking care with your grammar and spelling.

Questions 6 and 7

Improve your skills: finding key information
Study Question 6 and answer the following.

a What is the key word?
b Where do you remember it first being mentioned in the text?
c Which word in the same paragraph has a similar meaning?
d What does this word tell you about the answer?

▶ Check your answers on page 40 before you continue.

Answer the question below using NO MORE THAN THREE WORDS for each answer.

6 Where, apart from Earth, can space travellers find water? ....

7 What happens to human legs during space travel? ....

Scan the text for the sections where the topic of the question appears. The views expressed will probably be the writer's, unless there is reported or direct speech quoting somebody else.

Look for expressions with similar meanings to words in the statement.

Decide whether the writer agrees with the statement or not.

If you can't find any mention of the topic, 'not given' may be the answer.

Don't choose 'yes' or 'no' just because you believe it to be true.

Questions 8–12

Improve your skills: identifying the writer's views
1 Find a sentence in the text about the topic of Question 8. Who says this?
2 Match expressions in this sentence with these words. Remember that these expressions may not be the same part of speech as those in the statement.

| obstacles | far into space | medical |
| sending people | now … not | technological |

3 Find the paragraph relevant to Question 10. Who agrees with statement 10? How does the writer respond to this?

▶ Check your answers on page 40 before you continue.

Do the following statements agree with the writer's views in Reading Passage 1?

In boxes 8–12 on your answer sheet write

> **YES**   *if the statement agrees with the views of the writer*
>
> **NO**   *if the statement does not agree with the views of the writer*
>
> **NOT GIVEN**   *if there is no information about this in the passage*

8 The obstacles to going far into space are now medical, not technological.

9 Astronauts cannot survive more than two years in space.

10 It is morally wrong to spend so much money on space biomedicine.

11 Some kinds of surgery are more successful when performed in space.

12 Space biomedical research can only be done in space.

Look closely at the
headings and contents of
the table, particularly the
example line: it may not
be at the top. This shows
you how the information
is organized in the text.

Decide what the missing
information has in
common, e.g. people,
descriptions, or actions.

Decide how the answer
needs to be expressed,
e.g. as a complete phrase,
and what kinds of words
are needed, e.g. names,
adjectives + nouns, or
verbs + nouns.

The answers may or may
not be close together in
the text. For each
question, scan the text to
find it and fill in the space
without going over the
word limit.

Questions 13 and 14

Improve your skills: organization and expression
Study the table and the answer these questions.

a What does the table tell you about the organization of the text?
b What kind of information do you have to find?
c How should the answer be expressed? What kind of word is used?
d Compare the instructions 'Choose NO MORE THAN THREE WORDS from the
   passage', with those for short-answer questions on page 21. In what way are
   they different?

▶ Check your answers on page 40 before you continue.

Complete the table below

Choose NO MORE THAN THREE WORDS from the passage for each answer.

Write your answers in boxes 13 and 14 on your answer sheet.

Research area	Application in space	Application on Earth
Telemedicine	treating astronauts	13 .... in remote areas
Sterilization	sterilizing waste water	14 .... in disaster zones
Miniaturization	saving weight	wearing small monitors comfortably

Reading Passage 2

*You should spend about 20 minutes on **Questions 15–27**, which are based on Reading Passage 2.*

VANISHED
Who pulled the plug on the Mediterranean? And could it happen again?

By Douglas McInnis

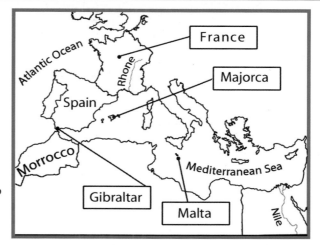

Cannes. Monte Carlo. St Tropez. Magic names all. And much of the enchantment comes from the deep blue water that laps their shores. But what if somebody pulled the plug? Suppose the Mediterranean Sea were to vanish, leaving behind an expanse of salt desert the size of India. Hard to imagine? It happened.

'It would have looked like Death Valley,' says Bill Ryan, from the Lamont-Doherty Earth
10 Observatory in New York, one of the leaders of the team that discovered the Mediterranean had once dried up, then refilled in a deluge of Biblical proportions. Between five and six million years ago, the great desiccation touched off what scientists call the Messinian Salinity Crisis – a global chemical imbalance that triggered a wrenching series of extinctions and plunged the Earth into an ice age.

The first indications of some extraordinary past events came in the 1960s, when geologists
20 discovered that major rivers flowing into the Mediterranean had eroded deep canyons in the rock at the bottom of the sea. River erosion of bedrock cannot occur below sea level, yet somehow the River Rhone in the South of France had managed to create a channel 1000 metres deep in the sea floor, while the Nile had cut nearly 1500 metres into the rock off the North African coast. There was more: despite the fact that the formation of caves can only take place above water, scientists
30 discovered a whole network beneath the island of Malta that reached an astonishing depth of 2000 metres below sea level.

Further evidence came to light in 1970, when an international team chugged across the Mediterranean in a drilling ship to study the sea floor near the Spanish island of Majorca. Strange things started turning up in core samples: layers of microscopic plants and soil sandwiched between beds of salt more than two kilometres below
40 today's sea level. The plants had grown in sunlight. Also discovered inside the rock were fossilized shallow-water shellfish, together with salt and silt: particles of sand and mud that had once been carried by river water. Could the sea floor once have been near a shoreline?

That question led Ryan and his fellow team leader, Kenneth Hsü, to piece together a staggering chain of events. About 5.8 million years ago, they concluded, the Mediterranean was gradually cut off
50 from the Atlantic Ocean when continental drift pinned Morocco against Spain. As the opening became both narrower and shallower, the deep outward flow from sea to ocean was progressively cut off, leaving only the shallow inward flow of ocean water into the Mediterranean. As this water evaporated, the sea became more saline and creatures that couldn't handle the rising salt content perished. 'The sea's interior was dead as a door nail, except for bacteria,' says Ryan. When the

60 shallow opening at Gibraltar finally closed completely, the Mediterranean, with only rivers to feed it, dried up and died.

Meanwhile, the evaporated water was falling back to Earth as rain. When the fresh water reached the oceans, it made them less saline. With less salt in it to act as an antifreeze, parts of the ocean that would not normally freeze began to turn to ice. 'The ice reflects sunlight into space,' says Ryan. 'The planet cools. You drive yourself into an ice age.'

70 Eventually, a small breach in the Gibraltar dam sent the process into reverse. Ocean water cut a tiny channel to the Mediterranean. As the gap enlarged, the water flowed faster and faster, until the torrent ripped through the emerging Straits of Gibraltar at more than 100 knots. 'The Gibraltar Falls were 100 times bigger than Victoria Falls and a thousand times grander than Niagara,' Hsü wrote in his book *The Mediterranean was a Desert* (Princeton University Press, 1983).

80 In the end the rising waters of the vast inland sea drowned the falls and warm water began to escape to the Atlantic, reheating the oceans and the planet. The salinity crisis ended about 5.4 million years ago. It had lasted roughly 400,000 years.

Subsequent drilling expeditions have added a few wrinkles to Ryan and Hsü's scenario. For example, researchers have found salt deposits more than two kilometres thick – so thick, some believe, that the Mediterranean must have dried up and 90 refilled many times. But those are just geological details. For tourists the crucial question is, could it happen again? Should Malaga start stockpiling dynamite?

Not yet, says Ryan. If continental drift does reseal the Mediterranean, it won't be for several million years. 'Some future creatures may face the issue of how to respond to nature's closure. It's not something our species has to worry about.'

Strategies: summarizing using words from the text

Check the instructions for the maximum number of words you can use.

Study the words before and after each gap and decide what kind of expression you need, e.g. preposition, noun phrase. Try to predict some of the missing words.

Look for the part of the text that the summary paraphrases and read it again.

Decide which sentence in the text probably corresponds to which question.

When you have filled in all the gaps, check your spelling and make sure the completed summary makes sense.

Improve your skills: predicting answers
Read the summary without referring back to the text.

a What part of speech is probably needed in each gap?
b Can you guess some of the words, or say what they might describe?

▶ Check your answers on page 40 before you continue.

Complete the summary below.

Choose NO MORE THAN THREE WORDS from the passage for each answer.

Write your answers in boxes 15–19 on your answer sheet.

The 1960s discovery of 15 ……………………… in the bedrock of the Mediterranean, as well as deep caves beneath Malta, suggested something strange had happened in the region, as these features must have been formed 16 ……………………… sea level. Subsequent examination of the 17 ……………………… off Majorca provided more proof. Rock samples from 2000 metres down contained both vegetation and 18 ……………………… that could not have lived in deep water, as well as 19 ……………………… originally transported by river.

Questions 20–22

Quickly try to guess the
endings from your first
reading of the text.

Decide what each stem
expresses, e.g. contrast,
condition, reason,
purpose, result.

Make a note of endings
that logically cannot fit
any of the stems.
Highlight the key words in
the remaining endings.

Remember that the stems
(but not the endings)
follow the order of
information in the text.

For each stem, search the
text for phrases with a
similar meaning. Then
look in that part of the
text for phrases similar to
one of the endings.

When you match an
ending, check the whole
sentence makes sense,
and that it means the
same as that part of the
text.

Improve your skills: eliminating impossible endings
Study questions 20–22 and options A–G.

a What does each of 20, 21, and 22 express? e.g. *contrast*.
b Which of A–G logically cannot fit each of 20–22?

▶ Check your answers on page 40 before you continue.

Complete each of the following statements with the best ending from the box below.

Write the appropriate letters A–G in boxes 20–22 on your answer sheet.

20 The extra ice did not absorb the heat from the sun, so …

21 The speed of the water from the Atlantic increased as …

22 The Earth and its oceans became warmer when …

A	Africa and Europe crashed into each other.
B	water started flowing from the Mediterranean.
C	the sea was cut off from the ocean.
D	all the fish and plant life in the Mediterranean died.
E	the Earth started to become colder.
F	the channel grew bigger, creating the waterfalls.
G	all the ice on earth melted.

Strategies: multiple-
choice questions

For each question study
the stem only, not A–D as
some of these might
mislead you.

Find the relevant part of
the text, highlight it and
read it again carefully.

Decide which of A–D is
closest in meaning to your
understanding of the text.

Look for proof that your
answer is correct and that
the rest of A–D are not.
Here are some common
types of wrong answer:

• It says something that
may be true but is not
mentioned in the text.

• It exaggerates what the
text says, e.g. it uses
words like *always* or *no
one*.

• It contradicts what the
text says.

• It contains words from
the text, or words with
similar meanings, but
about something else.

Questions 23–27

Improve your skills: identifying incorrect answers
Which of options A–D in question 23:

a says something that may be true, but is not mentioned in the text?
b contradicts what the text says?
c contains words from the text, but about something else?

▶ Check your answers on page 40 before you continue.

*Choose the appropriate letters **A, B, C** or **D** and write them in boxes 23–27 on your
answer sheet.*

23 What, according to Ryan and Hsü, happened about 5.8 million years ago?

    A Movement of the continents suddenly closed the Straits of Gibraltar.

    B The water level of the Atlantic Ocean gradually fell.

    C The flow of water into the Mediterranean was immediately cut off.

    D Water stopped flowing from the Mediterranean to the Atlantic.

24 Why did most of the animal and plant life in the Mediterranean die?

    A The water became too salty.

    B There was such a lot of bacteria in the water.

    C The rivers did not provide salt water.

    D The sea became a desert.

25 According to the text, the events at Gibraltar led to

    A a permanent cooling of the Earth.

    B the beginning and the end of an ice age.

    C the formation of waterfalls elsewhere in the world.

    D a lack of salt in the oceans that continues to this day.

26 More recent studies show that

    A Ryan and Hsü's theory was correct in every detail.

    B the Mediterranean was never cut off from the Atlantic.

    C it may have been cut off more than once.

    D it might once have been a freshwater lake.

27 At the end of the article, Ryan suggests that

    A the Mediterranean will never dry up again.

    B humans will have the technology to prevent it drying up again.

    C the Mediterranean is certain to dry up again one day.

    D humans will never see the Mediterranean dry up.

*You should spend about 20 minutes on **Questions 28–40**, which are based on Reading Passage 3.*

Dogs: a love story

A Genetic studies show that dogs evolved from wolves and remain as similar to the creatures from which they came as humans with different physical characteristics are to each other, which is to say not much different at all. 'Even in the most changeable mitochondrial DNA markers – DNA handed down on the mother's side – dogs and wolves differ by not much more than one per cent,' says Robert Wayne, a geneticist at the University of California at Los Angeles.

B Wolf-like species go back one to two million years, says Wayne, whose genetic work suggests dogs of some sort began breaking away about 100,000 years ago. Wolf and early human fossils have been found close together from as far back as 400,000 years ago, but dog and human fossils date back only about 14,000 years, all of which puts wolves and/or dogs in the company of man or his progenitors before the development of farming and permanent human settlements, at a time when both species survived on what they could scratch out hunting or scavenging.

C Why would these competitors cooperate? The answer probably lies in the similar social structure and size of wolf packs and early human clans, the compatibility of their hunting objectives and range, and the willingness of humans to accept into camp the most suppliant wolves, the young or less threatening ones.

D Certain wolves or protodogs may have worked their way close to the fire ring after smelling something good to eat, then into early human gatherings by proving helpful or unthreatening. As wandering packs of twenty-five or thirty wolves and clans of like-numbered nomadic humans roamed the landscape in tandem, hunting big game, the animals hung around campsites scavenging leftovers, and the humans might have used the wolves' superior scenting ability and speed to locate and track prospective kills. At night, wolves with their keen senses could warn humans of danger approaching.

E Times might not have been as hard back then as is commonly thought. In many instances food would have been plentiful, predators few, and the boundaries between humans and wildlife porous. Through those pores slipped smaller or less threatening wolves, which from living in packs where alpha bosses reigned would know the tricks of subservience and could adapt to humans in charge. Puppies in particular would be hard to resist, as they are today. Thus was a union born and a process of domestication begun.

F Over the millennia, admission of certain wolves and protodogs into human camps and exclusion of larger, more threatening ones led to the development of people-friendly breeds distinguishable from wolves by size, shape, coat, ears and markings. Dogs were generally smaller than wolves, their snouts proportionally reduced. They would assist in the hunt, clean up camp by eating garbage, warn of danger, keep humans warm, and serve as food. Native Americans among others ate puppies, and in some societies it remains accepted practice.

G By the fourth millennium BC Egyptian rock and pottery drawings show dogs being put to work by men. Then, as now, the relationship was not without drawbacks. Feral dogs roamed city streets, stealing food from people returning from market. Despite their penchant for misbehaviour, and sometimes because of it, dogs keep turning up at all the important junctures in human history.

H In ancient Greece, 350 years before Christ, Aristotle described three types of domesticated dogs, including speedy Laconians used by the rich to chase and kill rabbits and deer. Three hundred years later, Roman warriors trained large dogs for battle. The brutes could knock an armed man from his horse and dismember him.

I In seventeenth-century England, dogs still worked, pulling carts, sleds, and ploughs, herding livestock, or working as turn-spits, powering wheels that turned beef and venison over open fires. But working dogs were not much loved and were usually hanged or drowned when they got old. 'Unnecessary' dogs meanwhile gained status among English royalty. King James I was said to love his dogs more than his subjects. Charles II was famous for playing with his dog at Council table, and his brother James had dogs at sea in 1682 when his ship was caught in a storm. As sailors drowned, he allegedly cried out, 'Save the dogs and Colonel Churchill!'

J By the late nineteenth century the passion for breeding led to the creation of private registries to protect prized bloodlines. The Kennel Club was formed in England in 1873, and eleven years later the American Kennel Club (AKC) was formed across the Atlantic. Today the AKC registers 150 breeds, the Kennel Club lists 196, and the Europe-based Fédération Cynologique Internationale recognizes many more. Dog shows sprouted in the mid-1800s when unnecessary dogs began vastly to outnumber working ones, as they do to this day. Unless, that is, you count companionship as a job.

Read the text for gist, focusing on the key sentences, and think about how it is organized.

Study the questions and underline the key words. Remember that the questions are not in the same order as the information in the text.

Decide in which part of the text you are likely to find each answer, writing in any answers you can do from your first reading.

For the remaining answers, look more closely at the text for clues: words and phrases with similar or related meanings to the key words in the questions.

Questions 28–31

Improve your skills: locating answers

1 Quickly read the text. On what principle is it organized?

2 What are the key words in each of questions 28, 29, 30 and 31?

3 Which of questions 28–31 would you expect to find answered:
   a   near the beginning of the text?
   b   somewhere in the middle of the text?
   c   close to the end of the text?

▶ Check your answers on page 40 before you continue.

Reading Passage 3 has ten paragraphs labelled A–J.

Write the correct letters A–J in boxes 28–31 on your answer sheet.

28 Which paragraph explains how dogs became different in appearance from wolves?

29 Which paragraph describes the classification of dogs into many different types?

30 Which paragraph states the basic similarity between wolves and dogs?

31 Which paragraph gives examples of greater human concern for animals than for people?

Strategies: selecting from a list

Look at the four types of wrong answer in multiple-choice questions page 27.

Decide in which part of the text the statements are likely to be: they may not be in the same order as the information in the text.

Look for a paraphrase of each statement in the list, possibly in more than one part.

Lightly cross off the list any statements which are contradicted by the text.

Fill in the answers on your answer sheet in any order.

Questions 32–35

Improve your skills: finding references in the text

1 Which half of the text discusses
   a   wolves and early humans?
   b   dogs and early civilizations?

2 In which half will you probably find statements A–H?

3 Here are extracts from the text relating to statements A and B.

   A: 'the similar … size of wolf packs and early human clans'
   B: 'before the development of … permanent human settlements'

   For each, find a second reference to confirm your answer.

▶ Check your answers on page 40 before you continue.

Which **FOUR** *of the following statements are made in the text?*

Choose **FOUR** *letters from* **A–H** *and write them in boxes 32–35 on your answer sheet.*

A   In a typical camp there were many more wolves than humans.

B   Neither the wolves nor the humans lived in one place for long.

C   Some wolves learned to obey human leaders.

D   Humans chose the most dangerous wolves to help them hunt.

E   There was very little for early humans to eat.

F   Wolves got food from early humans.

G   Wolves started living with humans when agriculture began.

H   Early humans especially liked very young wolves.

Questions 36–40

Strategies: matching lists

Study the list of questions. For each one, highlight the key words.

Study the option list, e.g. of nationalities A–F. For each one, scan the passage for it and highlight that part of the text.

For each of A–F, ask yourself simple questions, e.g. 'Did the … use them to …?', and answer them by looking at the part you have highlighted. Look out for words similar to the key words in the question.

Remember that some of A–F may be used more than once or not at all.

Improve your skills: scanning the text

1   In which paragraph is each of A–F mentioned? Which nationality is mentioned in more than one paragraph? Which is not mentioned?

2   Ask yourself two questions about each of A–F.

▶   Check your answers on page 40 before you continue.

From the information in the text, indicate who used dogs in the ways listed below (Questions 36–40).

Write the correct letters **A–F** *in boxes 36–40 on your answer sheet.*

NB *You may use any letter more than once.*

Used by
A   the Greeks
B   the French
C   the Egyptians
D   the Romans
E   the English
F   the Native Americans

36   in war

37   as a source of energy

38   as food

39   to hunt other animals

40   to work with farm animals

Academic Writing   1 hour

Question Strategies: selecting main features from a graph, chart, or table

In Writing Task 1, you do not need to describe all the information given. To *summarize*, you must *select the main features* from what is shown.

Information is often given in the form of a graph, a chart, or a table.

Read any headings, key and sources for the data to understand what it relates to.

Read labels carefully, paying special attention to horizontal and vertical axes, column and row headings.

The data may show differences or changes over time, between places, or between groups of people. Try to identify significant contrasts, similarities, or trends.

The writing test consists of two tasks. You should attempt both tasks.

Writing Task 1

Improve your skills: understanding a graph

Study the graph below and think about the following.

a What is the overall topic?
b Look at the key for the four lines. Which groups of people are being compared? What do the numbers on the vertical axis show?
c What does the horizontal axis show?
d Can you identify a general trend in each graph? When was the trend most or least noticeable?
e Which period shows a deviation from the trend for some countries?

▶ Check your answers on page 41 before you continue.

You should spend about 20 minutes on this task.

The graph below shows four countries of residence of overseas students in Australia.

Summarize the information by selecting and reporting the main features, and make comparisons where relevant.

Write at least 150 words.

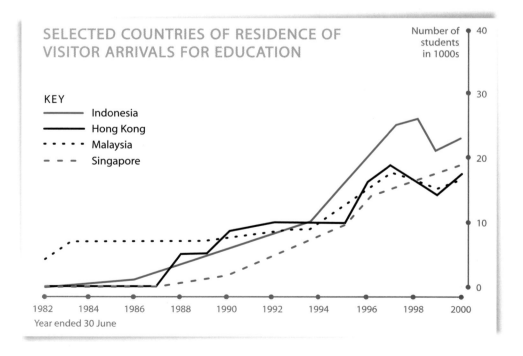

SELECTED COUNTRIES OF RESIDENCE OF VISITOR ARRIVALS FOR EDUCATION

Number of students in 1000s

KEY
—— Indonesia
—— Hong Kong
····· Malaysia
– – – Singapore

Year ended 30 June

Composition Strategies: reporting main features

Decide which points you will include and how you will organize them.

State the topic and overall content of the graph.

Describe and where relevant compare the main features of the data. Avoid repetition and do not try to give reasons.

Describe changes and trends using appropriate language: *the number rose/fell slightly/sharply, there was a steady/rapid increase/decrease in the number.*

Write numbers as percentages (*ten per cent*), fractions (*a quarter, two-thirds*), or expressions (*nine out of ten, three times as many*). Use approximate phrases such as *roughly, over, a little more than, just under.*

Conclude by outlining the overall trends.

Improve your skills: putting statistics into words

1 Choose the best way to express these statistics.

    a Put these percentages into words: 98%, 22.5%
    b State each of these fractions in two ways: 1/6, 4/5, 1/20
    c Compare each pair of numbers in two ways: 90 and 30, 17 and 34.
    d Write these numbers using approximate phrases: 51%, 999, 9.5%, 135.

2 Look at the graph in Writing Task 1. Describe the changes between 1982 and 1992 for the countries shown.

▶ Check your answers on page 41 before you continue.

Writing Task 2

You should spend about 40 minutes on this task.

Write about the following topic.

Air traffic is increasingly leading to more noise, pollution and airport construction. One reason for this is the growth in low-cost passenger flights, often to holiday destinations.

Some people say that governments should try to reduce air traffic by taxing it more heavily.

Do you agree or disagree?

Give reasons for your answer and include any relevant examples from your own knowledge and experience. Write at least 250 words.

Question Strategies: understanding the task

In Writing Task 2, you will be given a point of view to consider. You will be asked to give your opinion about the topic and the issues that are presented.

You are expected to *give reasons* for your answer and, where possible, support your arguments with *relevant examples*.

Read the statement in bold italics carefully to identify the general topic.

Decide which parts of the statement are fact and which are opinion.

Read the questions carefully and decide your views on the opinion expressed.

Improve your skills: identifying the topic and the issues

1   What is the general topic of the task?

2   Which part of the task is fact?

3   Which part of the task is opinion? How do you know?

4   Which part are you supposed to respond to? What is your view?

▶ Check your answers on page 41 before you continue.

Composition strategies: giving reasons and examples

Before you start writing, note down the issues raised by the title.

Decide your opinion on each issue and think of at least one argument to support it.

To illustrate each argument think of an example, perhaps from personal experience.

Use a separate paragraph to deal with each issue, its arguments and examples.

Improve your skills: developing arguments

Here are some issues raised by Writing Task 2. For each one answer *yes* or *no* and choose a supporting argument from the list. Then add an additional argument.

Example: 1 *No*

Supporting argument: g

Additional argument: overseas students also use these flights.

1 Is it fair?

2 Is it necessary?

3 Would it work?

4 Are there any alternatives?

5 Should governments get involved?

a tax rises would reduce demand

b air traffic growth essential to economy

c cleaner and quieter aircraft possible

d more and more cars despite high petrol taxes

e state interference always harms economy

f no other measures can curb air traffic growth

g poorer passengers would pay bill

h only the state can control polluting industries

i holiday travel not essential to economy

j aeroplanes even more polluting than cars

▶ Check your answers on page 41 before you continue

Speaking

Part 1

Strategies:
Part 1 questions

Listen for key words, e.g. studies, holidays, to help you understand the topic.

Give replies that are full (not just 'yes' or 'no'), relevant and addressed to the examiner.

Add relevant follow-up points, so that the examiner doesn't have to prompt you.

Remember that one aim of Part 1 is to help you relax by letting you talk about a familiar topic: yourself.

Improve your skills: predicting questions

Study the questions below, including the headings, e.g. *Where you grew up*. Note down some likely questions under each of these headings:

a   Friends
b   Reading books
c   Clothes and fashion

Answer the questions you have written.

▶ Check your answers on page 41 before you continue

You will be asked some general questions about a range of familiar topic areas. This part lasts between four and five minutes.

What is your full name?

What do people usually call you?

Where are you from?

Where you grew up.

1   What kind of town is it?

2   What's the most interesting area?

3   What kinds of jobs do people do there?

4   Do you think it's a good place to live?

What you do in your spare time.

5   Do you have any hobbies or interests?

6   How did you first become interested in that?

7   What other things like that would you like to do?

Travelling and transport.

8   What kinds of transport do you use regularly?

9   How do people in your country travel on long journeys?

10   How has transport there changed over the last twenty-five years?

Part 2

**Strategies:
planning Part 2**

Be prepared to describe
people, places, objects,
events, etc.– and to
explain their significance
to you personally.

Study the topic and
decide who or what you
are going to talk about.

Make brief notes for each
key word such as *who*,
what, *when*, *how* or *why*,
but don't try to write a
speech.

Before you begin
speaking, cross out
anything irrelevant.

Improve your skills: choosing relevant points

1 Which of these points are irrelevant to the topic in Part 2? Cross them out and
say what is wrong with each.

name	job	age now
born in my country	how I'll succeed	unchanged by success
often interviewed on TV	what is 'success'?	studied hard
now spoilt and arrogant	ordinary family	good role model
another successful person is	has failed at everything	overcame problems

2 Note down some relevant points of your own.

▶ Check your answers on page 41 before you continue

*You will be given a topic to talk about for one to two minutes. Before you talk, you
will have one minute to think about what you are going to say. You will be given
paper and a pencil to make notes if you wish. Here is the topic:*

> Describe someone you know, or somebody famous, who has achieved
> great success.
>
> You should say:
>
> who they are and what they do
>
> where they come from: their background
>
> how they became successful
>
> and explain why you admire this person.

Follow-up questions:

Has this person had to make sacrifices in order to achieve success?

Do most people in your country share your admiration for him/her?

Part 3

Strategies:
Part 3 questions

Expect a link between the topics of Part 2 and Part 3.

Listen for the key words in the examiner's questions.

Be sure you understand the question. If not, ask for repetition.

Think about what the examiner wants you to do in response to each question, e.g. speculate, contrast, make a comparison or suggestion.

Don't expect the examiner to ask you about something else if you can't think of anything to say. Think harder!

Develop the discussion by adding more points linked to the topic.

Improve your skills: adding more ideas

To develop the topic of question 1 in Part 3, you could talk about qualifications, money, possessions, appearance, titles, prizes, fame, etc.

Note down at least five points you could mention in answer to question 2.

▶ Check your answers on page 41 before you continue

You will be asked some questions about more abstract issues and concepts related to the topic in Part 2. This discussion lasts between four and five minutes.

Personal success

1   How does present-day society measure the success of an individual?

2   How can we ensure that more people achieve their aims in life?

3   Would you rather be successful in your job or in your social life?

Winning and losing

4   Which is more important in sport: winning or taking part?

5   What makes some sports people take drugs to improve their performance?

6   Why are some countries more successful than others in events such as the Olympics?

The competitive society

7   How do competitive relationships between people differ from cooperative relationships?

8   In what ways has society become more competitive in the last twenty years?

Test 1 Improve your skills key

Listening

Focusing on speakers page 10
a   a customer and shop assistant; to ask for / give information
b   either both in the shop or speaking by phone
c   conversational
d   numbers, bicycle vocabulary, methods of payment

Understanding the task page 11
a   letters
b   write in three names
c   Woods Road, Oak Street, the park, the police station, the pharmacy

Identifying main features page 11
a   the police station
b   on the other side of the street, on the opposite corner
c   on the other side of the street, facing, opposite
d   10

Predicting from examples page 12
12   social
14   charities / charitable
16   political / politics

Predicting from stems page 13
18   *In this city, clubs and societies are mainly paid for by*: the financing of clubs
19   *Finding the right club might influence your choice of*: the relevance of clubs to important personal decisions
20   *What should you do if the right club does not exist?*: how to find the right club for you

Looking for clues page 14
a   the imperative; the sentences are making suggestions and giving advice (including the answer to 23)
b   note form – articles, possessives, etc., can be left out.

Identifying key words page 15
26   where, sit, attend
27   do, miss, point
28   why, notes, easy, read
29   which expressions, coming next

Question forms page 15
a   28
b   29
c   26
d   27

Describing diagrams page 15
a   page, text, margin, top, bottom, left (-hand side), right (-hand side)
b   Similarities: they all have text filling the centre of the page, they all have space around
Differences: summing-up points at top/in left margin/at bottom/in right margin
c   sheet (of paper), writing, space, gap, room, above, below, under, alongside, next to

Understanding the overall meaning page16
a   Australia
b   opal mining
c   in the late 1940s, due new opal fields and mass immigration
d   below ground to avoid the extreme climate; buildings underground include churches and hotels

What kind of word? page 16
31   a number
32   a year
33   an historical event
34   a part of the world
35   a percentage
36   a building

Thinking of synonyms page 17
1   B: near
    C: far from
2   in: *not outside, centre, downtown, urban*, etc
    near: *nearby, close to, not far from, just beyond, not far off, a short distance from, neighbouring*, etc
    far from: *far-off, distant, far away, a long way from, further, a great distance*, etc.

Reading

Identifying key sentences page 18
A, B, C, D, E, G   first sentence
F   second sentence

Focusing on examples page 18
Paragraph A describes space biomedicine, beginning with the topic sentence: 'Space biomedicine is …', and then states its aims.
Although the first sentence of paragraph F mentions ethical and financial issues, this is not the theme of the paragraph. The second sentence introduces ways that space biomedical research can help resolve problems on Earth.

Finding key information page 21
a   water
b   the second sentence of paragraph B
c   ice
d   there is a link with 'Mars'

Identifying the writer's views page 21
1   In paragraph B, the sentence beginning 'This involvement of NASA …'. The writer says this. There are no reporting verbs, quotes or references to what others say.
2   obstacles: limited, constraints
      sending people: travel
      far into space: to other planets, and beyond
      now…not: no longer
      medical: what the human body can actually withstand
      technological: engineering
3   Pargraph F. The writer does not say who agrees exactly: 'Such considerations have led *some* to question the ethics …'. The writer contrasts this with his/her own opinion: 'It is now clear, however, …'

Organization and expression page 22
a   There are practical applications of different research areas: first in space and then on Earth.
b   human activities: applications on Earth of telemedicine and sterilization.
c   as part of an incomplete phrase or sentence; -ing form of verbs plus noun phrases
d   Unlike the table instructions, the open questions do not specify from the passage.

Predicting answers page 25
a   15   noun (plural or uncountable) or noun phrase
      16   preposition
      17   noun or noun phrase
      18   noun (plural or uncountable)
      19   noun (plural or uncountable)
b   15   something found under the sea
      16   at/above/below
      17   something in or under the water
      18   something living that is not vegetable, i.e. animal
      19   possibly something that is neither vegetable nor animal, i.e. mineral

Eliminating impossible endings page 26
a   20   a reason
      21   a result
      22   a result
b   20 G   21 C   22 E

Identifying incorrect answers page 27
a   B
b   A
c   C

Locating answers page 30
1   It is organized chronologically: from pre-history to the present day.
2   28   dogs, different appearance from wolves
      29   classification, dogs, types
      30   similarity, wolves, dogs
      31   greater human concern, animals
3   a   30
      b   28
      c   29, 31

Finding references in the text page 30
1   a   first half
      b   second half
2   probably in first half.
3   A   'packs of 25 or 30 wolves and clans of like-numbered … humans'
      B   'wandering packs … and … nomadic humans roamed'

Scanning the text page 31
1   Greeks   H
      French   no mention
      Egyptians   G
      Romans   H
      English: I, J
      Native Americans   F
2   e.g. Did the Greeks use dogs? If so, how/in what way?

Writing

Understanding a graph page 32
a   Where overseas students in Australia come from.
b   Students from four countries: Indonesia, Malaysia, Hong Kong, Singapore. The vertical axis shows students numbers.
c   The time scale over which comparisons can be made.
d   After a slow start, the figures for all four countries have risen sharply. The numbers from Indonesia have grown fastest; those from Malaysia slowest.
e   There is a dip in the mid 1990s.

Putting statistics into words page 33
1   a   ninety-eight per cent, twenty-two and a half per cent
    b   one sixth, one in six, one out of six; four-fifths, four in five, four out of five; one twentieth, one in twenty, one out of twenty.
    c   three times as many / the number of, one third as many / the number of, half as many / the number of, twice /double the number of
    d   a little / just over / roughly half; almost exactly / just under a thousand; less than / just under / fewer than ten percent; well over a hundred
2   Suggested answers:
    The number of students from Malaysia rose steadily between 1982 and 1992.
    There was a rapid increase in the number of students from Hong Kong between 1982 and 1992.

Identifying the topic and the issues page 34
1   increasing air traffic
2   the first part is fact
3   the second part is opinion because of the phrase 'some people say that'
4   the second part

Developing arguments page 35
1   yes (i)   no (g)
2   yes (j)   no (b)
3   yes (a)   no (d)
4   yes (c)   no (f)
5   yes (e)   no (h)

Speaking

Predicting questions page 36
a   Do you have many friends? How did you first meet them? Do you have a best friend? When do people become friends? Do you find it easy to make new friends? What are the advantages of having friends? Why do friends sometimes fall out?
b   What kind of books do you like? Which book have you enjoyed most? Where and when do you usually read books? What makes a good book? Which authors are popular in your country? Will people continue to read books in the future?
c   What are your favourite clothes? Do you prefer any particular colour(s)? What is currently fashionable in your country? How have fashions changed in the last 5 years? What do you think will be fashionable in the next 5 years? Where do fashions come from?

Choosing relevant points page 37
1   how I'll succeed (it's not about you)
    what is 'success'? (discussion of abstract topics is in Part 3)
    now spoilt and arrogant (not a reason for admiring them)
    another successful person is (you can only talk about one)
    has failed at everything (wrong person to talk about)
2   Suggested answers: went to local school, worked seven days a week, does charity work, provides jobs for hundreds of people, always polite.

Adding more ideas page 38
Suggested answers: elimination of unemployment and poverty; improved education; equal opportunities irrespective of race, gender, religion, etc; better facilities for the disabled; improved careers advice; more resources for the arts, sports, etc; better health care at all ages.

Test 2

Listening 30 minutes

Section 1

Strategies: classification

Before you listen, look at the words in capitals and think of other ways of saying the same thing.

When the recording is played, listen for these expressions and others like them. They can tell you which letter to circle.

Think about the intonation. This may indicate the speaker's attitude.

Questions 1–6

Improve your skills: words used to classify

The words in capitals under Classification can be of various types. Note down other ways of saying each of the following.

a Always recommended, e.g. *suggest in every case, should at all times*
  sometimes recommended
  never recommended

b in favour
  no opinion either way
  against

c yes, definitely
  maybe
  definitely not

▶ Check your answers on page 71 before you continue.

How does the owner answer? Write

A *if she says YES, DEFINITELY*

B *if she says MAYBE*

C *if she says DEFINITELY NOT*

| *Example*   House free of damp?   *Answer* B |

1   Current gas safety certificate? ....

2   Gas inspection within last twelve months? ....

3   Electricity checked in last five years? ....

4   Sufficient electric sockets? ....

5   Fire detection equipment that works? ....

6   Previous tenants all returned keys? ....

**Strategies:
questions with figures**

Before you listen, think about how numbers in the questions are pronounced. This makes them easier to recognize when you hear them. You could write them out too, e.g. 70 m = seventy metres.

Make sure you know what they relate to, e.g. length of bridge, depth of water.

Listen for these numbers. Take care with numbers which are similar but don't relate to the question.

For clues to total numbers, listen for expressions like *plus, too, as well as, another, a third one*, etc.

Questions 7–10

Improve your skills: recognizing numbers

1 How are these pronounced? Write them out in words.

2/3	7/10	0.615	the 80s	32nd	43rd
54th	101st	50%	454 BC	1066 AD	16 mm
5 cm	220 km	33 C°	25 mg	1800 cc	300 m²

2 Study questions 7–10. What kind of figure is needed for each?

▶ Check your answers on page 71 before you continue

Circle the correct letters A–D.

7 On which floor is the storeroom?

   A first

   B second

   C third

8 What is the temperature of the hot water?

   A 55°

   B 60°

   C 70°

9 How big is the garden?

   A 20 m²

   B 90 m²

   C 150 m²

10 What size is the television?

   A 70 cm

   B 80 cm

   C 90 cm

Section 2

Strategies: questions about charts

Before you listen, look at the chart and its headings, key, scale, etc., and decide what it shows.

Ask yourself questions about the main features.

When the recording is played, study the diagrams and listen for words such as *study*, *survey*, or *findings* that may introduce statistics.

Listen for numbers and for expression used to describe variations in numbers, e.g. *a big gap between*, *a sharp rise in*, and approximations, e.g. *just over a third of*. Be careful with figures that seem right but may be used in the wrong context.

Answer while you listen. Don't try to remember lots of numbers and decide later.

Questions 11 and 12

Improve your skills: understanding data

1   What is the purpose of the three charts in Question 11?

2   Ask yourself a question about each chart and answer it, e.g. *What percentage of students suffered from loneliness according to A? Sixteen per cent.*

3   Repeat 2 above for Question 12.

▶   Check your answers on page 71 before you continue.

Choose the correct letters A–C

11   Which column of the chart shows the percentage of young people suffering loneliness?

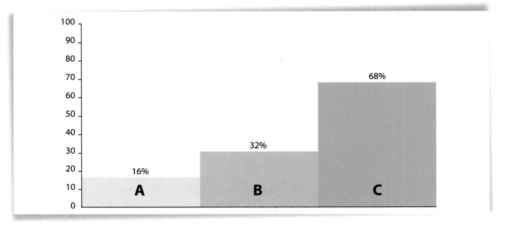

12   Which chart shows the percentage of young people using the counselling service?

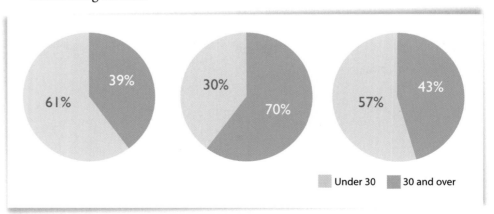

Strategies: completing sentences

Before you listen, underline the key words in each sentence and decide what you need to write, e.g. a verb, a number, a noun phrase.

Listen for the key words, or phrases with similar meanings.

Write in words you hear, or words of your own with similar meanings

After you listen, check your answers make logical and grammatical sense – you are completing sentences, not notes.

Questions 13–20

Improve your skills: using the right kind of word

Read the sentences in Questions 13–20. What kinds of words must you use in each?

▶ Check your answers on page 71 before you continue.

Complete the sentences below.

Write NO MORE THAN THREE WORDS for each answer.

Many young people feel lonely during their 13 .... away from home.

You may feel lonely even though you are often with 14 ....

People may find it easier to adapt if they have been 15 .... before.

It's possible you last needed to make new friends at 16 ....

Someone special to you may live 17 .... from you.

Don't forget that 18 .... is affected by loneliness.

Doing interesting 19 .... is a good way to meet new people.

The 20 .... at your town hall can tell you more about counselling.

Section 3

**Strategies:
multiple answers**

Read *Strategies: multiple-choice questions* on page 13.

Before you listen, check how many answers you must give. If two answers are needed for one question, you need both to get one mark.

Keep listening after you hear an answer: the next answer may follow soon after.

After you listen, check you have given the correct number of answers to each question.

Questions 21–23

Improve your skills: understanding the question
For each each task between 21 and 30 answer these questions.

a How many options are there?
b How many answers must you give?
c Are there separate marks for each answer, or one mark for two correct answers?

▶ Check your answers on page 71 before you continue.

Circle THREE letters A–F.

What does Katy say about the Language Centre?

    A   It is near the College.

    B   The library's materials are for advanced learners only.

    C   All books have accompanying cassettes.

    D   It receives a Spanish newspaper every day.

    E   At present, at least fifteen languages are taught by computer.

    F   All the computers can be used for Internet learning.

Question 24

Choose TWO letters A–E.

Which TWO of the following can you watch on the second floor?

    A   live TV in English

    B   live TV in Japanese

    C   live TV in Turkish

    D   recorded news in Arabic

    E   recorded news in Portuguese

Questions 25–27

*Circle THREE letters **A–F**.*

What must you do when you join the Language Centre?

A   pay a small amount of money

B   show some proof of identity

C   be accompanied by someone from your Department

D   take a test in the language you want to study

E   register at Reception in the Language Centre

F   learn how to use the Centre's equipment

Questions 28

*Choose TWO letters **A–E**.*

Which TWO should you tell the librarian?

A   whether you have studied the language previously

B   why you want to study this language

C   how many hours per week you must study it

D   which text books you will use

E   which other languages you have learned

Questions 29–30

*Circle TWO letters **A–E**.*

Which TWO of these can you do at the Language Centre?

A   read and listen to materials on your own

B   choose books to take away from the Centre

C   copy tapes to listen to them outside the Centre

D   photocopy materials yourself

E   have a few pages of a book photocopied

Section 4

Questions 31–34

Strategies: completing notes and tables

Look at any examples: studying these can make you feel more confident about doing the task when you hear the recording.

For each question, make sure you understand what kind of information you may have to write in and where.

Think about words that often go with the kind of word you need. For example, if you decide the answer is a time of day, you might first hear *at*, *before* or *after*.

Improve your skills: listening for lexical clues

Decide what kind of information is needed for each of 31–34, e.g. a year.

Think of – or find in the notes – a word likely to go with each, e.g. a year: *in* 2010.

▶ Check your answers on page 71 before you continue.

Look at the table.

Write NO MORE THAN TWO WORDS OR A NUMBER for each answer.

The Zip Fastener				
1851	Howe	'Automatic Continuous Clothing Closure'	commercial potential only	USA
1893	Judson	'Clasp Locker'	commercial failure	31 USA
1908	Sundback	'Hookless Fastener'	commercial 32	Sweden
33	Kynoch	'Ready Fastener'	commercial success	UK
1920s	34	'Zipper'	commercial success	USA

Look at the title and think of real life examples of the object.

Decide from which angle you are looking at the diagram, e.g. from one side.

Describe the diagram to yourself, identifying all the parts.

Think about how the speaker will describe it and what phrases you might hear. If you can guess any answers already, pencil them in.

Listen out for prompts that tell you the description is about to start, e.g. *In the drawing you'll see …*, *As shown in …*.

Follow the question numbers on the diagram, e.g. from left to right or clockwise, and write your answers as you hear them.

Questions 35–39

Improve your skills: predicting a description

Study the diagram and answer the questions.

a From what angle are you looking at the zip?
b What vocabulary do you know for what you can see?
c What other words or phrases do you think you will hear?
d In what order do you think you will hear the information?

▶ Check your answers on page 71 before you continue.

Label the zip. Write NO MORE THAN THREE WORDS for each answer.

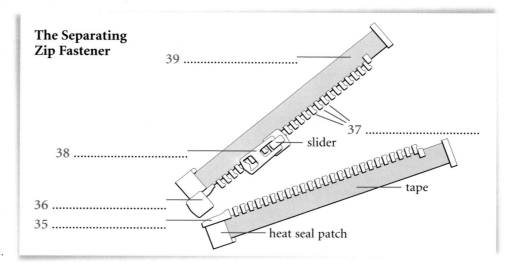

The Separating Zip Fastener

39 ....

37 ....

slider

38 ....

tape

36 ....

35 ....

heat seal patch

Strategies: global questions

Identify the global question: it is often the last of several multiple-choice items.

Decide what it is testing, e.g. *What is the lecturer trying to do?* means you have to identify the speaker's purpose.

Think about how the language and tone might differ for each option.

When you listen, reject options that misinterpret what the speaker means, relate to only part of the content, or overstate it.

Question 40

Improve your skills: predicting global features

1 Study the first line of question 40. What is its focus?

2 Study A–D. What language features and speaker's tone would you expect for each?

▶ Check your answers on page 71 before you continue

Choose the correct letter, A, B, C or D.

40 The speaker's overall aim is to

A explain how different kinds of zip fastener work.

B outline the development of the zip fastener.

C advertise a particular kind of zip fastener.

D warn of the dangers of zip fasteners.

Academic Reading   1 hour

Reading Passage 1

*You should spend about 20 minutes on **Questions 1–14**, which are based on Reading Passage 1.*

Scratching the surface

They are insidious skin parasites, infesting the occupants of factories and offices. They cause itching, prickling and crawling sensations in the skin that are almost untreatable. These creatures may only exist in the mind, but their effects are real and infectious.

The classic case occurred in a US laboratory in 1966. After new equipment was installed, workers started to suffer from itching and
10 sensations of insects crawling over them. Complaints multiplied and the problem, attributed to 'cable mites', started to spread to relatives of the victims. A concerted effort was made to exterminate the mites using everything from DDT and mothballs to insecticide and rat poison.

Nothing worked. Thorough examination by scientific investigators could not locate any pests, or even signs of actual parasite attacks. However,
20 they did find small particles of rockwool insulation in the air, which could cause skin irritation. A cleaning programme was introduced

and staff were assured the problem had been solved. The cable mite infestation disappeared.

Another 1960s case occurred in a textile factory, where workers complained of being bitten by insects brought into the factory in imported cloth. Dermatitis swept through the workforce, but it followed a curious pattern. Instead of affecting people in one particular part 30 of the factory, the bugs seemed to be transmitted through employees' social groups. No parasites could be found.

A third infestation spread through office staff going through dusty records that had lain untouched for decades. They attributed their skin problems to 'paper mites', but the cause was traced to irritation from paper splinters.

These are all cases of illusions of parasitosis, where something in the environment is 40 misinterpreted as an insect or other pest. Everyone has heard of delirium tremens, when alcoholics or amphetamine users experience the feeling of insects crawling over their skin, but other factors can cause the same illusion. Static electricity, dust, fibres, and chemical solvents can all give rise to imaginary insects. The interesting thing is that they spread. The infectious nature of this illusion seems to be a type of reflex 50 contagion. Yawn, and others start yawning. If everyone around you laughs, you laugh. Start scratching, and colleagues will scratch, too.

* Dr Paul Marsden is managing editor of the Journal of Memetics, the study of infectious ideas. He suggests that this type of group behaviour may have had a role to play in human evolution. In our distant past, one individual scratching would have alerted others that there were biting insects or parasites present. This would prime 60 them to scratch itches of their own. Anyone who has been bitten several times by mosquitoes before they realized it will recognize the evolutionary value of this kind of advance warning. The outbreak of mass scratching may also promote mutual grooming, which is important in the necessary bonding of primate groups.

The problem comes when the reflex contagion is not related to a real threat. 70 Normally, everyone would soon stop scratching, but people may unconsciously exaggerate symptoms to gain attention, or because it gets them a break from unappealing work. The lab workers were scanners, who spent the day laboriously examining the results of bubble-chamber tests; textile workers and clerical staff poring over records would also have found what they had to do quite tedious. Add the factor that skin conditions are notoriously susceptible to psychological influence, and it is easy to see how 80 a group dynamic can keep the illusory parasites going.

Treatment of the condition is difficult, since few will accept that their misreading of the symptoms is the result of what psychologists call a hysterical condition. In the past, the combination of removal of irritants and expert reassurance was enough. However, these days, there is a mistrust of conventional medicine and easier access to support groups. 90

Sufferers can reinforce each other's illusions over the Internet, swapping tales of elusive mites that baffle science. This could give rise to an epidemic of mystery parasites, spreading from mind to mind like a kind of super virus. Only an awareness of the power of the illusion can stop it.

You can stop scratching now ...

Read *Strategies: matching lists* on page 31.

Strategies: classifying statements

Read *Strategies: matching lists* on page 31.

Instead of people or places, there is a list of statements: these may not follow the order of the text.

If more than one answer is possible, write them both in.

Questions 1–5

Improve your skills: finding the relevant section
Which paragraphs focus on

   a   the laboratory?
   b   the factory?
   c   the office?

Which paragraph mentions all three? Is it relevant to any of questions 1–5?

▶ Check your answers on page 72 before you continue.

Classify statements 1–5 according to whether they apply to

   A   the laboratory

   B   the factory

   C   the office

1   Workers who met each other socially suffered from the condition.

2   The victims were all working with old documents.

3   They tried to kill the insects they thought were responsible.

4   They said the creatures had come in material from abroad.

5   Employees' families were affected by the condition.

Read *Strategies: short-
answer questions* on
page 21.

Look at how the flow
chart is organized: arrows
often indicate results,
stages or changes. Count
the number of these
points.

Find the part of the text
that relates to the chart.
Look for the same number
of points and identify the
relationship between
them, e.g. linking words
like *Firstly* and *Next*
indicate a sequence.

Ask yourself questions
about the text, e.g. *What
happens next?*, and match
the answers with the
points in the chart.

Questions 6–8

Improve your skills: understanding links between ideas

1 Study the text and answer these questions.
   a   What is the immediate consequence of the bite?
   b   What are the two immediate results of this?
   c   What can be the immediate effect of group scratching?
   d   What can this in turn lead to?

2 Study the flow chart and answer these questions.
   a   What do the arrows mean?
   b   What kind of information is needed for 6?
   c   What kind of information is needed for 7 and 8?

▶ Check your answers on page 72 before you continue.

Complete the notes below with words taken from Reading Passage 1.

Use NO MORE THAN TWO WORDS for each answer.

Evolutionary purpose theory

parasite / insect bite

↓

6 .... → benefit to group:
7 ....
to presence of pests

↓

group scratching

↓

group grooming → benefit to group:
8 ....

Strategies: *true/false/not given* **questions**

Read *Strategies: yes/no/not given* questions on page 21. Note that *true/false/not given* questions focus on facts in the text, whereas *yes/not/not given* questions are often about the writer's opinions.

If you can't find any mention of the topic, 'not given' may be the answer.

Don't choose 'true' or 'false' just because you believe it to be true.

Questions 9–13

Improve your skills: finding clues

Study questions 9 and 10 carefully and answer these questions.

a What does the adverb 'unconsciously' (line 71) tell you about the answer to 9?
b Which adverb and which adjective are clues to the answer to 10?

▶ Check your answers on page 72 before you continue

In boxes 9–13 on your answer sheet write

> **TRUE**   *if the statement is true according to the passage*
>
> **FALSE**   *if the statement is false according to the passage*
>
> **NOT GIVEN**   *if the statement is not given in the passage*

9   Some keep scratching because they know it will enable them to stop work.

10 The laboratory, factory and office employees all had boring jobs.

11 The human skin is extremely sensitive to irritants.

12 In many cases, people no longer believe what medical professionals say.

13 It is impossible to prevent the condition becoming an Internet epidemic.

Strategies: choosing a title

After you have done all the other tasks, sum up the whole text in a few words.

Look at the titles and decide which is closest to your own words. Ignore any which:

• are based on an overall misunderstanding of the text.

• are too narrow, i.e. cover only part of the text.

• are too broad, i.e. cover aspects of the topic beyond the scope of the text.

Question 14

Improve your skills: eliminating incorrect titles

1 Study the five titles A–E. Which one:
   a   is based only on some of the early paragraphs?
   b   focuses only on the last part of the text?
   c   only covers the information in the paragraph marked * ?
   d   mentions topics that are beyond the scope of the text?

2 Why is the other title correct?

▶ Check your answers on page 72 before you continue

From the list below choose the most suitable alternative title for Reading Passage 1.

Write the appropriate letter A–E in box 14 on your answer sheet.

A   The benefits of itching and scratching

B   Increasing complaints about insects

C   Scratching, yawning and laughing

D   Imaginary bites and parasites

E   Computer bites and Internet itches

Reading Passage 2

*You should spend about 20 minutes on **Questions 15–27**, which are based on Reading Passage 2.*

Strategies: matching headings to sections

Read *Matching headings to paragraphs* on page 18. Substitute *section* for *paragraph*.

Don't choose headings that match only one paragraph in a section, or more than one section.

Questions 15–19

Improve your skills: eliminating incorrect headings

1 Why is example f correct?

2 Which of headings a–j is wrong because it:

    a   covers more than one section?

    b   focuses only on the first thing in the text?

    c   only covers one paragraph?

    d   exaggerates what the text says?

▶ Check your answers on page 72 before you continue

*Reading Passage 2 has six sections **I–VI**.*

*Choose the most suitable heading for each section **II–VI** from the list below. Write the appropriate letters (**a–j**) in boxes 15–19 on your answer sheet.*

List of headings
a   The lift in use
b   The first and second lifts
c   Restoring the lift
d   The new canal
e   Mechanical problems
f   Why the lift was needed
g   The supports of the second lift
h   A new framework and machinery
i   How the original lift worked
j   A completely new lift

Example   Section I   Answer   f

15 Section II

16 Section III

17 Section IV

18 Section V

19 Section VI

The Anderton Boat Lift

❧ Section I

When the Trent and Mersey Canal opened in 1777, the Cheshire town of Anderton was the obvious place to transfer goods to and from the nearby River Weaver. There was just one problem: the canal was fifteen metres above the river.

Pathways, inclined planes, and chutes were constructed to ease the task of moving cargo by hand. Primitive railways were laid to move cargoes, cranes were built, and steam engines were later installed to power lifting. In the early 1870s, however, the Weaver Navigation Trustees decided to eliminate the cost, effort, and wastage involved in hand transportation when the engineers Edward Leader Williams and Edwin Clarke suggested a 'boat carrying lift'.

❧ Section II

Their design was a unique and magnificent example of the Victorians' mastery of cast iron and hydraulics. Completed in 1875, graceful in appearance, simple in use, and above all efficient, the lift was hailed as a marvel of the era, and became a prototype for larger versions on the waterways of France and Belgium.

The operating mechanism consisted of two vertical sets of interconnected hydraulic cylinders and pistons set into the bed of the river and each piston supported a boat-carrying tank 22.86 metres long and 4.72 metres wide. At rest, one tank was level with the canal and the other level with the river and to move the tanks, a small amount of water was removed from the bottom tank making it lighter than the top tank.

Because the two hydraulic cylinders were connected, the heavier top tank moved down and forced hydraulic liquid through the connecting pipe into the other cylinder pushing that piston and the lighter tank upwards. Watertight gates both on the tanks and at the entrance to the canal contained the water while the tanks were moving. A hydraulic pump driven by steam supplied the small amount of additional energy required to effect a reasonably rapid movement and to enable the tanks to be precisely levelled at the end of their journey.

❧ Section III

All went well for the first ten years, then pitting and grooving of the cylinders and pistons occurred. Investigations showed that the canal water used as the hydraulic liquid was contaminated by chemicals and was corrosive, therefore causing the damage.

It was immediately changed to distilled water from the steam engine powering the hydraulic pump. Corrosion was dramatically reduced but the damage had been done.

In addition, the boiler for the steam engine needed renewing, so in 1906 the Trustees ordered the construction of a new lift, to a design by their engineer J A Saner.

❧ Section IV

The new lift was built over the top of the Victorian structure, utilizing the Victorian front and rear columns. The main structure had strong A-frames at either side of the new lift to support the enormous weight of the platform that now formed the top of the framework: on it was located the new operating mechanism, which included seventy-two pulleys weighing up to 35 tonnes each.

Each of the boat-carrying tanks was now suspended on wire ropes which ran from the tank to the top of the lift, around pulleys, and down to cast-iron weights at the side of the structure. These were equal to the weight of the water-filled tank. Turning the pulleys one way or the other moved the ropes, so that one tank was raised or lowered independently of the other tank. Because the tanks were counterbalanced by the weights, only a small electrical motor was required to turn the pulleys and so move the tanks up or down.

Completed in 1908 the lift was reliable, cheap and easy to operate. Unlike the Victorian lift it was not the least bit elegant, but it was functional and it worked.

❧ Section V

Both the 1875 the 1908 versions carried large volumes of commercial traffic and the principal cargoes transported were coal, china clay, salt, manufactured goods, including china ware, and agricultural produce.

Sadly, trade on inland waterways in Britain declined dramatically in the 1950s, and goods traffic via the lift effectively ended in the 1960s. The 1970s increase in pleasure boating briefly prolonged its active life, but in 1982 the 'Cathedral of the Canals' was finally closed.

❧ Section VI

Demolition seemed inevitable, but, after a long campaign by concerned groups, British Waterways agreed, in 1999, to save the lift.

Some wanted it 'conserved as found', but that would entail replacing much of the existing structure, virtually creating a replica lift. The steel of the 1908 structure had been badly corroded by pollutants from the local chemical industries and would need replacing if it were to support the overhead machinery and 500-tonne counterweights. In addition, safety considerations would require the installation of a back-up braking system.

It was decided, therefore, to revert to the 1875 hydraulically-operated system, using the original cast-iron structure. Although the counterweights had to be removed, the 1908 framework and pulleys would be retained as a static monument.

It was a huge and expensive project, and not without difficulties. Eventually, in 2002, the Anderton Boat Lift was officially reopened. Boat owners and visitors alike can once again ride 'the world's first boat lift'.

When you have read the
text, study the diagram
and the labels given.
Decide which part of the
text describes it. Pencil in
any answers you can
guess already.

Match the information in
the diagram to what the
text says. To understand
how the parts relate to
each other, look for links
of purpose, e.g. *to/in order
to/so as to* + infinitive, and
result, e.g. *-ing, and/so/so
that*.

When you have written in
your answers, go through
the text again to check
that everything matches
the completed labels.

Questions 20–24

Improve your skills: understanding how something works

1 Look at Section II and answer these questions.
   Examples:
   Why was a small amount of water … removed?   Answer: *to move the tanks.*
   What was the result of this?   Answer: *making it lighter.*
   a   What was the result of forcing *hydraulic liquid … into the other cylinder*?
   b   Why was *additional energy* supplied? What was the purpose of this?
        Give two examples.

2 Find 2 purpose and 2 result links in Section IV. Ask and answer a question
   about each.

▶ Check your answers on page 72 before you continue.

Complete the diagram below.

Choose NO MORE THAN THREE WORDS from the passage for each answer.

Write your answers in boxes 20–24 on your answer sheet.

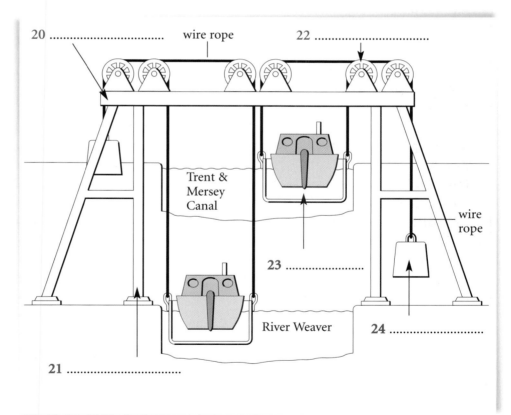

20 .... wire rope 22 ....

Trent &
Mersey
Canal

wire
rope

23 ....

River Weaver 24 ....

21 ....

Study each question and
decide what is needed,
e.g. a noun phrase, a
number.

In your mind, try to turn
the notes or sentences
into questions and then
answer them. This should
give you the missing
words.

Check your completed
sentences make sense
and paraphrase what the
text says.

Questions 25–27

Improve your skills: forming questions

1 For each of 25–27, decide what kind of answer is needed.
2 Form a question from each, e.g. *Where were similar lifts later built?*, and answer
  it.

▶ Check your answers on page 72 before you continue

Complete the notes below

*Choose NO MORE THAN THREE WORDS from Reading Passage 2 for each
answer.*

Write your answers in boxes 25–27 on your answer sheet.

25 Similar lifts to the Anderton were later built in ....

26 Extra power to move the tanks came from ....

27 Using water from the canal harmed the ....

Reading Passage 3

*You should spend about 20 minutes on **Questions 28–40**, which are based on Reading Passage 3.*

Life, but not as we know it

Henry Gee

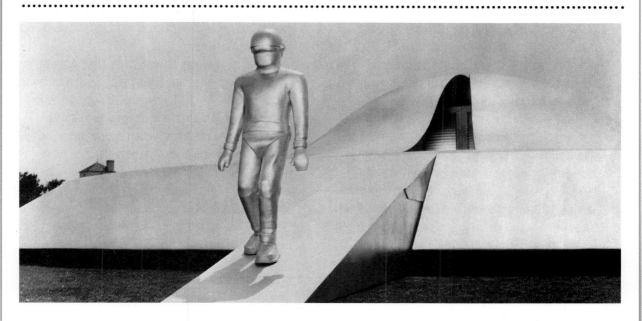

Astrobiology is arguably the trendiest buzzword in science after genomics. Like genomics, it is as hip as it is hard to define. Broadly speaking, it is an umbrella term for the efforts of many scientists working in diverse fields to understand the conditions of life in the universe, whether on Earth or elsewhere.

The canvas is, in fact, so broad that many scientists might be astrobiologists without knowing
10 it: astrobiology adds glamour to all science, from astronomy to zoology. Those with long memories and a cynical mien will have seen all this before. Once upon a time, there was a research programme called exobiology. Is astrobiology a new name for repackaged goods?

No, for two reasons. First, many discoveries made in the past decade have set people thinking, once again, about life elsewhere. For example, hardly a month goes by without the discovery of
20 yet another planet orbiting a distant star. And whatever the truth about the much-disputed claims for fossils in martian meteorites, the controversy has rehabilitated the idea of panspermia: that life can spread between planets.

Second, astrobiology is almost a trademarked term. The Nasa Astrobiology Institute is a virtual campus linking research centres with universities, all devoted to learning more about the general principles governing the origin of life in the
30 universe. Significantly, Nature magazine recently looked at astrobiology in all its forms, from the quest to understand how life began on Earth to the prospects of finding intelligent life elsewhere in the universe.

Not that this should be a cause for wide-eyed celebration, say its critics. Ironically, the most vociferous of these come not from the world of science but from science fiction. Brian Aldiss, veteran writer, critic, and leading light of the genre,

40 dismisses our current obsession with life elsewhere, however much it is justified by science, as an expensively scratched itch.

Aliens, he argues, are a manifestation of a fundamental human urge to populate the universe with 'others', whether gods, ghosts, little green men, or cartoon characters. Scientists should beware of taking science fiction too seriously: aliens are useful as plot devices, but this does not make them real.

50 A rather different criticism comes from scientists-turned-science fiction writers Jack Cohen and Ian Stewart. Both are academics – Cohen is a biologist, Stewart is a mathematician – but they have worked in SF, most recently on their novel *Wheelers*. Their argument with astrobiology is not that aliens might not exist, but that we cannot help be constrained in our search.

All organisms on Earth, from the tiniest bacterium to the biggest whales, are constructed

60 according to the same rules. Earthly genetic information is carried in genes made of DNA, earthly life is based on polymers of carbon, and its chemistry happens in liquid water. Because this kind of life is all we know, we tend to think that the same rules need apply everywhere. So, when probes land on Mars, or scientists look at martian meteorites, they tend to look for the kinds of vital signs that betray earthly organisms when we have absolutely no reason for thinking that life elsewhere

70 should be earthlike, or that our definition of life cannot be based more broadly. When the Mars Rover sat and stared at a rock, how do we know that the rock was not staring right back?

It is a fairly simple matter to come up with a definition of life that is based on what it does, rather

than what it is made of. It is much more difficult, however, to make such a definition stick, preventing the term from becoming so inclusive as to be meaningless.

80 You might start by positing three rules. The first is that life requires the existence of information that can be reproduced and inherited, with variation. Second, that living systems seem to create order and structure and maintain it in the face of chaos. Third, that a living system has to work hard to maintain its structure, and as soon as it stops doing this it degenerates.

These rules seem, at first, to be fairly precise, in as much they weed out quietly observant martian

90 surface rocks. But as Cohen and Stewart show in their novel, it is possible to imagine entities that follow all three rules and which appear to be alive, but which bear absolutely no resemblance to terrestrial organisms. In *Wheelers*, they describe civilizations of floating, methane-breathing balloons in the atmosphere of Jupiter and organisms made of magnetically-confined plasma, living in the outer layers of the sun.

Other science fiction writers have imagined life

100 on the surfaces of neutron stars, inside computers, or even in interstellar space. In his latest novel, *Look to Windward*, Iain M Banks describes organisms the size of continents, supporting entire civilizations as their intestinal parasites. All could be said to constitute life, but in Dr McCoy's immortal phrase from Star Trek, 'not as we know it'.

Could this mean that astrobiology, the aims of which are universal, is really no more than a parochial exercise? We might never know – perhaps

110 even when we are visited by aliens from the other side of the galaxy who try, frantically, to gain our attention, by waving under our noses whatever it is they wave under such circumstances. It will not be their fault that they will be microscopic and destroyed by a single sneeze. As Cohen and Stewart conclude in *Wheelers*: 'Life goes on everywhere.'

Read *Strategies:
summarizing using words
from the text* on page 25,
but remember that words
in a list are not usually
taken directly from the
text.

Decide what part of
speech is needed for each
gap.

Mark the words in the list
according to their part of
speech, e.g. adverb,
singular noun.

Match each with at least
one other word of the
same part of speech that
has a related meaning.
They could be synonyms,
near-synonyms, or
opposites.

For each gap, try the
words that fit
grammatically and
logically – not the whole
list.

Questions 28–34

Improve your skills: finding words that fit

1 What parts of speech are needed for 28–34? e.g. 0 – *plural noun*
2 What parts of speech are the words in the list? e.g. *principles – plural noun*
3 Which other words in the list form pairs in some way with a–f below?
   e.g. *principles – regulations*

   a   location
   b   basing
   c   frequently
   d   galaxy
   e   definition
   f   mistake

► Check your answers on page 72 before you continue

*Complete the summary below. Choose the answers from the box and write the
corresponding words in boxes 28–34 on your answer sheet. There are more choices
than spaces, so you will not need to use all of them.*

The same biological and chemical 0 ....*principles*....... determine the make-up

of all terrestrial life forms, whatever their 28 .... We often

assume that this is the case throughout the universe, as we have

29 .... observed other kinds of organism. Scientists therefore

make the 30 .... of searching for indications of Earth-style

living things when examining material from another 31................................... ,

where the nature of any life may lie far outside their own 32 ....

definition. On the other hand, if the focus is not on 33 .... but

on behaviour, there is a risk of 34 .... life much too broadly.

List of words

location	principles	previous
narrow	galaxy	frequently
discussing	rarely	defining
never	composition	size
definition	planet	extending
mistake	breakthrough	
basing	regulations	

In this task, you must match speakers with the opinions they state. Expect the first reference to each person to include their full name and possibly other details; after that it is usually just their surname.

Look for reporting verbs such as *suggests*, and expressions that introduce opinions such as *their belief is that ... or according to ...* .

Questions 35–38

Improve your skills: finding opinions

1 In what order does the text mention Aldiss, Banks, and Cohen/Stewart?

2 Which expressions introduce the opinions of:
   a   Aldiss?
   b   Banks?
   c   Cohen & Stewart?

▶ Check your answers on page 72 before you continue

*The text refers to the ideas of various science fiction writers. Match writers **A–C** with the points in 35–38*

Write your answers in boxes 35–38 on your answer sheet.

You many use any of the writers more than once.

35   Other life forms may fit a definition of life but be quite unlike anything on Earth.

36   People instinctively want to believe in extraterrestrial life forms.

37   There could be life within life on an immense scale.

38   Humans are inevitably limited in their ability to find life beyond Earth.

List of writers
A   Aldiss
B   Banks
C   Cohen & Stewart

Scan the text for stylistic
devices such as these.

- **Rhetorical questions**
  intended to persuade
  the reader, e.g. What
  proof is there? They may
  or may not be answered
  in the text.

- **Adverbs** that make the
  writer's opinion clear,
  e.g. *fortunately, allegedly.*

- **Expressions** that show
  the writer's attitude, e.g.
  *be that as it may, without
  any doubt.*

- **Irony**: saying the
  opposite of what is
  meant, e.g. *this great
  success* (= total failure).

Questions 39–40

Improve your skills: interpreting the writer's techniques

1 Which sentences in the text correspond to each of A–D in Question 39? Which
   of these sentences contain:

   a   expressions that show the writer's attitude?
   b   a rhetorical question? How is it answered?
   c   an adverb that indicates the writer's opinion?

2 What do these taken together tell you about the purpose of the text?
   - the title
   - the mention of critics and criticism early in two paragraphs
   - the rhetorical question and its answer in the last paragraph

▶ Check your answers on page 72 before you continue

*Choose the appropriate letters **A–D** and write them in boxes 39–40 on your answer
sheet.*

39   The writer believes that astrobiology

   A   may now be the second most fashionable science.

   B   is very similar to exobiology.

   C   has proved that a meteorite from Mars contains fossils.

   D   is not taken seriously by scientific publications.

40   Which of the following statements best describes the writer's main purpose
     in Reading passage 3?

   A   to describe the latest scientific developments in the study of the universe

   B   to explain why there is growing interest in the study of astrobiology

   C   to show that science fiction writers have nothing useful to say about
        aliens

   D   to suggest that astrobiology may not help us find extraterrestrial life

Academic Writing   1 hour

The writing test consists of two tasks. You should attempt both tasks.

Writing Task 1

You should spend about 20 minutes on this task.

The diagram below shows the environmental issues raised by a product over its life cycle.

Summarize the information by selecting and reporting the main features, and make comparisons where relevant.

Write at least 150 words.

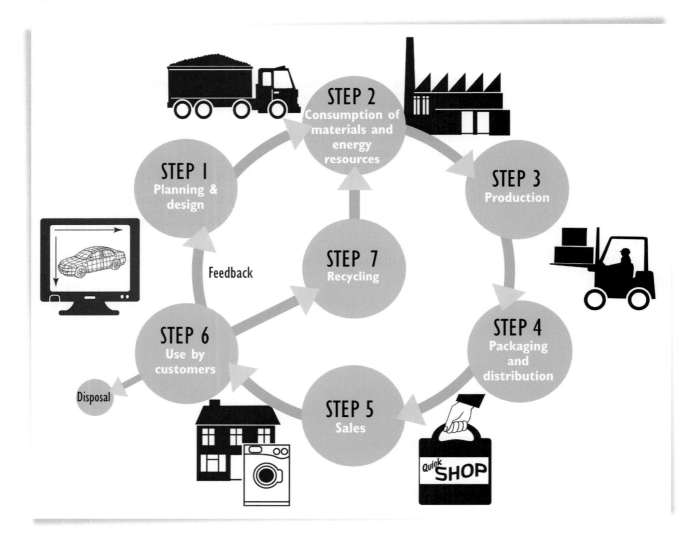

Question Strategies: selecting main features from a diagram

Information is sometimes given in the form of a diagram. Look quickly at this to form an overall impression of the topic.

Read labels carefully to understand what each element or stage of the diagram relates to.

In the case of a process, pay special attention to the direction of arrows. Check whether the process has a logical beginning and end.

Remember that in Writing Task 1 you only have to report the *main features*, not everything you can see.

Composition Strategies: reporting a process

Decide how you will organize your text. Begin by saying what the diagram shows.

Take all your information from the diagram, using your own words where possible.

To show the stages, use linking expressions, e.g. *to begin with, then, in the end.*

When you finish, check you have described all the *main features* of the diagram.

Improve your skills: understanding a diagram

Answer these questions about the diagram.

a What does it show?
b How many stages/steps are there?
c What do the arrows tell you?
d What kinds of negative impact on the environment are shown?
e What measures to reduce this impact are shown?

► Check your answers on page 73 before you continue

Improve your skills: organizing and linking ideas

Answer these questions about your writing before you start.

a At what step should you start?
b What verb tense should you use?
c In which part – the beginning, the main body or the ending – would you probably use these linking expressions?

meanwhile	finally	next	simultaneously
at this point	alternatively	initially	eventually
from there	ultimately	first	at the same time

► Check your answers on page 73 before you continue.

Writing Task 2

You should spend about 40 minutes on this task.

Write about the following topic:

Many people are using credit cards or loans to run up huge personal debts that they may be unable to repay. It should therefore be made more difficult for individuals to borrow large amounts of money.

What are your opinions on this?

Give reasons for your answer and include any relevant examples from your own knowledge and experience.

You should write at least 250 words.

Improve your skills: beginnings and endings

1 You can use some of techniques a–h in your Introduction or Conclusion. Match them with example expressions i–viii below.

Introduction

a Introduce the topic in your own words.
b Say why it is controversial
c State your position.
d Say how you will deal with the topic.

Conclusion

e Summarize the arguments you have used.
f Make concessions to opposing arguments.
g State or restate your position.
h Make a recommendation for the future.

i On balance, therefore, there seems to be agreement that …
ii I believe that steps should now be taken to ensure …
iii Although it cannot be denied that …
iv I shall compare and contrast the views …
v For these reasons, I feel there is little doubt that …
vi Recently, there has been considerable discussion of …
vii I do not find this statement at all convincing …
viii The implications of this have led some to claim that …

2 Note down more expressions you could use for a–h.

3 Look at the topic of Writing Task 2.
   a   What are your feelings about this?
   b   Which approach will you choose?
   c   Which of a–h above will you use?

▶ Check your answers on page 73 before you continue.

Composition Strategies: giving reasons

Guide your reader through your text by using linking expressions that show how your ideas are organized. To do this, use adverbials at the beginning of sentences.

Example

Firstly, *there can be no doubt that this substance brings no health benefits whatsoever, as shown by the government report.* ***There is also the fact that*** *it is far too expensive, compared with similar products.*

Improve your skills: linking points

In which part of a paragraph would you use these linking expressions?

Put them into these three groups.

a For the first point ....
b For subsequent points ....
c For the last point ....

Secondly	Finally	First of all	Moreover
In addition	Lastly	Besides	Furthermore
In the first place	Above all	To begin with	

▶ Check your answers on page 73 before you continue.

Speaking

Part 1

Strategies: speaking in Part 1

Avoid breakdowns in communication by using some or all of these strategies.

- Ask the examiner to repeat something, e.g. *I'm sorry but I didn't catch that.*
- Clarify if what you've just said is not clear, e.g. *What I'm saying is …*
- Hesitate, giving yourself time to think, e.g. *It's difficult to say exactly, but …*
- Correct mistakes you've made, e.g. *I got here a year ago, I mean an hour ago.*
- Describe approximately if you don't know the name, e.g. *… or that kind of thing.*
- Paraphrase, using other words to explain, e.g. *It's what you use to make …*

Improve your skills: communication strategies

Say which communication strategy is used in the expressions in italic. Then match sentences a–f with questions in Part 1.

a   I won't have milk, or cheese, *or anything like that.*
b   *Well, er, let me see …* yes, there was a story on the radio the other day.
c   We all live with my grandfathers; *sorry, what I meant was* my grandparents.
d   *Sorry, but I missed the word before* 'together'.
e   I sometimes have lunch in *one of those places where* you serve yourself.
f   *The point I'm making is* there's much less there about politicians' private lives.

▶ Check your answers on page 73 before you continue

You will be asked some general questions about a range of familiar topic areas. This part lasts between four and five minutes.

What is your full name?

What do people usually call you?

Where are you from?

Your family.

1   Is your family small or quite large?

2   What do you do when you are all together?

3   Which of them do you get on with best? Why?

Food and eating.

4   What are your favourite foods?

5   Is there anything you never eat?

6   Where do you normally eat? Why?

7   In what ways are people's eating habits changing these days?

The news media.

8   Where do you normally get your news from?

9   How do you think news reporting in your country differs from that abroad?

10   Tell me about an interesting news item you've read or heard recently.

Part 2

**Strategies:
speaking in Part 2**

Use your notes as
prompts while you speak,
not as a script.

Remember what you're
being tested on: fluency
and coherence,
vocabulary, range and
accuracy of grammar,
pronunciation.

Remember that you can
use less formal language
than in IELTS Writing.

Try to make what you say
interesting, as you would
in any other situation.

Give brief answers to the
follow-up questions at
the end.

Improve your skills: linking expressions

Put three of these expressions under each of the headings below.

And it's not only …	More importantly, …
To sum up …	The … I'd like to talk about is …
Take … for instance, …	So, what I'm saying is …
In a word, then, …	As well as that, …
A case in point is …	To illustrate this point, …
I've decided to speak about …	There are quite a lot of …, but the one I've chosen is …

Introducing the topic Developing the topic Giving examples Concluding your talk

► Check your answers on page 73 before you continue.

You will be given a topic to talk about for one to two minutes. Before you talk, you will have one minute to think about what you are going to say. You will be given paper and a pencil to make notes if you wish. Here is the topic:

Describe a music video or a concert that has made an impression on you.

You should say:
  which kind of music it was and who performed it
  what it was like musically
  what it was like visually
  and explain why you liked or disliked it.

Follow-up questions:

When and where did you see it?

Have you ever seen anything else similar to it?

Part 3

Strategies: speaking in Part 3

Give extended replies to every question, demonstrating your fluency.

Show your ability to discuss abstract topics, as you may need to do in tutorials.

Remember there are no right or wrong answers. It is a test of language – not of your opinions.

Improve your skills: saying what you think

Complete the table with suitable headings and your own examples.

Express opinions:	As I see it …, In my view …, To my mind …
...........................:	The reason is …, For one thing …,
Speculate:	I wouldn't be surprised if …,
...........................:	We don't we …?, How about …?,
Say you're sure:	I've no doubt that …,
...........................:	I can't say for certain, but …,
Compare/contrast:	On the one hand …,
...........................:	I'd rather … than …,

▶ Check your answers on page 73 before you continue.

You will be asked some questions about more abstract issues and concepts related to the topic in Part 2. This discussion lasts between four and five minutes.

Music in the world

Why is pop music so popular globally?

Which do you prefer: traditional music from your country or classical music from abroad?

The psychology of music

How do different kinds of music affect the way people feel?

What is the best music to listen to while studying?

Changes in music

What are the main differences between music today and that of previous decades?

Which contributes more to the success of modern singers and bands: their music, or their appearance and image? Why do you think so?

What kinds of music will people be listening to ten years from now?

Test 2 Improve your skills key

Listening page 42
Words used to classify
1 **b** may be advisable to, could make sense to, possibly a good idea to

   c shouldn't ever, on no account, warn against, in no circumstances,

2 **a** for, supporting, to back, in agreement with, argue for

   b open-minded, wouldn't like to say, undecided, can't make my mind up

   c opposed to, reject, not happy with, disagree with, don't go along with

3 **a** of course, absolutely, without question, for sure

   b possibly, perhaps, I'm not sure, I'll have to check, I'll let you know

   c certainly not, absolutely not, never, nobody, there's no question

Recognizing numbers page 43
1 **Top line**: two-thirds; seven-tenths; nought point six one five; the eighties; thirty-second, forty-third

   Middle line: fifty-fourth; a/one hundred and first; fifty per cent; four fifty four BC; ten sixty six AD, sixteen millimetres

   Bottom line: five centimetres; two hundred and twenty kilometres; thirty-three degrees Centigrade; twenty-five milligrams, eighteen hundred CC; three hundred square metres

2 ordinal number, degrees, square metres, centimetres

Understanding data page 44
1 The charts show the percentage of young people suffering loneliness.
2 What percentage of people suffered from loneliness according to B? 32%.
   What percentage of people suffered from loneliness according to C? 68%.
3 The charts show the percentage of young people using the counselling service.
   What percentage of users in each chart were under 30 / 30 and over?
   A   61% under 30, 39% 30 and over
   B   30% under 30, 70% 30 and over
   C   57% under 30, 43% 30 and over

Using the right kind of word page 45
13 noun/noun phrase
14 noun/noun phrase
15 adjective
16 noun/noun phrase
17 adverb(s)/preposition(s)
18 noun/noun phrase
19 noun (uncountable or plural)
20 noun/noun phrase

Understanding the question page 46
21–23 6 options; 3 answers; separate marks
24 5 options; 2 answers; one mark for two answers
25–27 6 options; 3 answers; separate marks
28 5 options; 2 answers; one mark for two answers
29–30 5 options; 2 answers; separate marks

Listening for lexical clues page 48
31 a country, *in*
32 a noun, *commercial*
33 a year, *in*
34 a name (of an inventor or designer), *invented/designed/made/created by*

Predicting a description page 49
a facing it, or above it

b *fastener, zipper, cloth, fabric, material, metal*, etc.

c Descriptive expressions, e.g. *on the left-hand side, at the top, the end*. Process expressions, e.g. *to join, to close, to open, to pull up/down.*

d First a description of the parts, then of how they work together.

Predicting global features page 49
1 The main purpose of the speaker.
2 A   Contrast links (whereas, on the other hand, etc), detailed description. Measured/neutral tone.

   B   Historical detail (dates, places, names, etc), time links, description. Academic/neutral tone.

   C   Focus on one type/brand, selected details, superlatives, exaggeration. Confident/enthusiastic tone.

   D   Giving advice (take care not to, remember to, you shouldn't, etc). Serious/concerned tone.

Reading

Finding the relevant section page 51
a the laboratory: lines 7–16, lines 17–24
b the factory: lines 25–33
c the office: lines 34–39
all three places: lines 68–82 (this is not relevant to questions 1–5)

Understanding links between ideas page 52
1 **a** someone starts scratching
   b others are alerted to the presence of biting pests; others start scratching too
   c others start grooming each other
   d bonding of the group
2 **a** cause and effect
   b a human activity
   c 7 a positive consequence of answer 6
      8 a positive consequence of group scratching and grooming

Finding clues page 53
a It implies the opposite of 'they know', so 9 is probably false.
b The words 'laboriously' and 'tedious' both indicate something 'boring', so 10 is probably true.

Eliminating incorrect titles page 53
a B
b E
c A
d C
D reflects the texts broad concern with people imagining infestations.

Eliminating incorrect headings page 54
1 The first section of Section I deals with the difference in water levels, attempts to overcome this difficulty and why they were unsatisfactory.
2 **a**: Heading b **c**: Heading g
   b: Heading d **d**: Heading j

Understanding how something works page 57
1 **a** pushing the piston and the lighter tank upwards.
   b to effect a reasonably rapid movement, to enable the tanks to be precisely levelled
2 Purpose links: Why did the main structure have strong A-frames? To support the platform / Why was a small electrical motor required? To turn the pulleys.
   Result links: What was the result of moving the ropes? One tank was raised or lowered / What was the result of turning the pulleys? The tanks moved up or down.

Forming questions page 58
1 25 place names
   26 noun/noun phrase
   27 noun/noun phrase
2 25 France and Belgium
   26 Where did extra power to move the tanks come from? a hydraulic pump.
   27 What did using water from the canal harm? The cylinders and pistons.

Finding words that fit page 61
1 28 noun
   29 adverb
   30 noun
   31 singular noun
   32 adjective
   33 plural or uncountable noun
   34 -ing form of verb
2 & 3 plural nouns: *principles/regulations*,
   singular nouns: *composition/definition*, *size/location, mistake/breakthrough, planet/galaxy*
   adjectives: *previous/narrow*
   adverbs: *never/rarely/frequently*
   -ing form of verbs: *defining/basing/extending*

Finding opinions page 62
1 Aldiss, Cohen & Stewart, Banks, Cohen & Stewart.
2 **a** Aldiss: 'dismisses'; 'he argues …'
   b Banks: 'In …, Banks describes …'
   c Cohen & Stewart: 'Their argument … is not that … but…'; 'as Cohen and Stewart show in …'; 'in … they describe …'; 'As Cohen and Stewart conclude in …'

Interpreting the writer's techniques page 63
1 **A** 'Astrobiology is arguably the trendiest buzzword in science after genomics.'
   B 'Is astrobiology a new name for repackaged goods? No, for two reasons.'
   C 'And whatever the truth about the much disputed claims for fossils in martian meteorites.'
   D 'Significantly, Nature magazine recently looked at astrobiology in all its forms.'
      a C: 'whatever the truth', 'much-disputed claims'
      b B: 'Is astrobiology a new name for repackaged goods? No, for two reasons.'
      c A: 'Astrobiology is *arguably* the trendiest buzzword in science after genomics.'
2 They convey the scepticism that he and others feel about astrobiology's chances of success in finding alien life.

Writing

Understanding a diagram   page 65

1   The impact on the environment of a manufactured product during its life cycle.
2   Seven main steps
3   What each step leads to.
4   The use of energy and resources at step 2; transport to step 3; factory production at step 3; packaging, printing & distribution (transport) at step 4; sales at step 5 (shops); use at step 6 followed by disposal (scrapped material & discharge), also involving storage (domestic appliances). Possibly also product planning & design at 1 (office).
5   Recycling from step 7 to step 1; less impact on environment at production step 3. Possibly also informing customers at step 5; service and repair at step 6; providing feedback for planning & design – steps 6 and 1.

Organizing and linking ideas   page 65

a   Step 1 (product planning & design)
b   Present simple
c   Beginning: *initially, first*
    Main body: *meanwhile, simultaneously, at this point, alternatively, from there, at the same time.*
    Ending: *finally, eventually, ultimately*

Beginnings and endings   page 66

1
	Introduction		Conclusion
a	vi	e	i
b	viii	f	iii
c	vii	g	v
d	iv	h	ii

2   a   A topic of great public debate at present is …
    b   The danger of this, according to … is …
    c   To a certain extent I agree with this, but …
    d   In this essay, I shall present evidence that …
    e   To sum up, it is clear that …
    f   Despite the undoubted advantages of this, …
    g   In view of the above, I strongly believe that …
    h   I would suggest that a change in the law is necessary in order to …

Linking points   page 67

a   *to begin with, in the first place, first of all*
b   *secondly, furthermore, moreover, in addition, besides, what*
c   *Finally, Lastly*

Speaking

Communication strategies   page 68

a   describing approximately, question 5
b   hesitating, question 10
c   correcting mistake, question 1
d   asking the examiner to repeat, question 2
e   paraphrasing, question 6
f   clarifying, question 9

Linking expressions   page 69
Introducing the topic
I've decided to speak about …; The … I'd like to talk about is …; There are quite a lot of …, but the one I've chosen is … .
Developing the topic
… and it's not only …; More importantly, …; As well as that, …
Giving examples
Take … for instance, …; A case in point is …; To illustrate this point.
Concluding your talk
To sum up …; In a word, …; So, what I'm saying is … .

Saying what you think   page 70
Justify opinions: *It's because …*
(Speculate:) *You can't rule out the possibility that, There may well be*
Suggest: *Why not…?*
(Say you're sure:) *I'm positive that, I'm quite convinced that*
Say you're not sure: *I don't really believe that, There must be some doubt as to*
(Compare/contrast:) *X is far better than Y, Whereas X …, Y …*
Express a preference: *X appeals to me far more than Y, My preference would be for*

Test 3

Listening 30 minutes

Section 1

Questions 1–6

What does Lisa say about each object?

Complete the table as follows. Write

    A *if she says it is ESSENTIAL.*

    B *if she says it is RECOMMENDED.*

    C *if she says it is NOT RECOMMENDED.*

Example	Documents	*Answer*	**A**

1   At least £50   ....

2   Warm clothing   ....

3   Personal computer   ....

4   Food from home   ....

5   Favourite tapes or CDs   ....

6   Photos from home   ....

Questions 7–10

Complete the sentences below.

Write NO MORE THAN THREE WORDS for each answer.

The labels on Dan's luggage must state 'Mr & Mrs 7 ....' and their address.

Lisa says he should carry some spare clothes in 8 ....

For health reasons, Dan intends to wear 9 .... during the flight.

Dan should practise carrying his luggage for a minimum distance of 10 ....

Section 2

Questions 11–13

Choose THREE letters A–F.

What does Sally say about universities?

A   Compared to the general population, few students are disabled.

B   Most universities don't want students aged over 25.

C   Old universities can present particular difficulties for the disabled.

D   All university buildings have to provide facilities for the disabled.

E   There are very few university disability advisors.

F   Some disability advisors can do little to help disabled students.

Questions 14–19

Complete the table below.

Write NO MORE THAN THREE WORDS for each answer.

Disability	Facilities
General	personal care and assistance
Mobility impairment	ramps and easy access, fire and emergency procedures 14 ...... lift .... lavatory facilities
15 ...... lavatory	induction loops, flashing sirens, 16 ...... visul door bell ......
Sight impairment	Braille translators, 17 ...... clear markings ...... on stairs, floors, etc fire and emergency procedures
Dyslexia	use of computer 18 ...... extra time ...... to finish work
Other difficulties	access to treatment: medication/therapy 19 .... procedures

Question 20

Choose the correct letter A, B, C or D.

20 What is the speaker's main purpose?

    A   to explain why comparatively few students are disabled

    B   to advise disabled students what to look for in a university

    C   to describe the facilities for the disabled in a particular university

    D   to criticize the facilities for the disabled in most universities

Section 3

Questions 21–26

Complete the notes below using letters A–F from the box.

NB   *You may use any letter more than once.*

A   tour of the university campus

B   formal dinner party

C   meeting with 'senior' students

D   driving in this country

E   visit to a night club

F   tour of the city

Orientation Course for international students

What Liz liked about the course.

21 .....C......

22 .....B......

23 .....F......   D

What Mark thinks could be improved.

24 .....A.....

25 .....C......

26 ....

Questions 27–30

Choose the correct letters A, B, C, or D.

27 Your room during the Orientation Course is

    A   usually shared with another student.

    B   the same room you will have for the rest of the year.

    C   some distance from the university.

    D   furnished, and with bedclothes provided.

28 The daytime temperature will probably be

    A   less than 10°C.

    B   between 10°C and 20°C.

    C   20°C.

    D   more than 20°C.

29 How much free email time do you get?

    A   30 minutes

    B   20 minutes

    C   15 minutes

    D   10 minutes

30 There are Orientation Course activities from

    A   Sunday to Saturday.

    B   Sunday to Friday.

    C   Monday to Friday.

    D   Monday to Saturday.

Section 4

Questions 31–33

Complete the sentences below.

Write NO MORE THAN TWO WORDS for each answer.

Fireworks were first used in China, probably in the 31 ....*6*......... century.

By the following century, they were known in Arabia as 32 .....*chinese aerials*.....

Fireworks first appeared in 33 .....*Europe*..... in the thirteenth century.

Questions 34–37

Label the diagram. Write NO MORE THAN THREE WORDS for each answer.

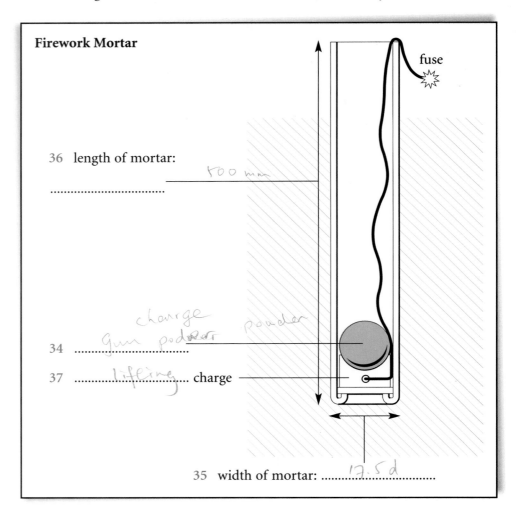

Firework Mortar

fuse

36 length of mortar:

....   *500 mm*

34 ......*Gun powder*......   *chaurge*   *powder*

37 ......*lifting*...... charge

35 width of mortar: .....*17.5 d*.....

Questions 38–40

Choose the correct letters A, B, C or D.

38 A multibreak shell

    A   is more dangerous than a simple shell.

    B   may make a noise when it bursts.

    C   has a single fuse for all its sections.

39 An aerial heart shape is made by the explosion of

    A   stars placed inside a shell in the form of a circle.

    B   heart-shaped stars placed inside a shell.

    C   stars arranged in the form of a heart inside a shell.

40 What does a Serpentine shell look like in the sky?

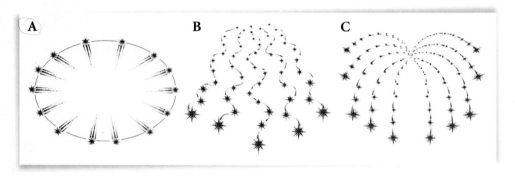

Academic reading   1 hour

Reading passage 1

*You should spend about 20 minutes on **Questions 1–14**, which are based on Reading Passage 1.*

Unmasking skin

A If you took off your skin and laid it flat, it would cover an area of about twenty-one square feet, making it by far the body's largest organ. Draped in place over our bodies, skin forms the barrier between what's inside us and what's outside. It protects us from a multitude of external forces. It serves as an avenue to our most intimate physical and psychological selves.

B This impervious yet permeable barrier, less than a millimetre thick in places, is composed of three layers. The outermost layer is the bloodless epidermis. The dermis includes collagen, elastin, and nerve endings. The innermost layer, subcutaneous fat, contains tissue that acts as an energy source, cushion and insulator for the body.

C From these familiar characteristics of skin emerge the profound mysteries of touch, arguably our most essential source of sensory stimulation. We can live without seeing or hearing – in fact, without any of our other senses. But babies born without effective nerve connections between skin and brain can fail to thrive and may even die.

D Laboratory experiments decades ago, now considered unethical and inhumane, kept baby monkeys from being touched by their mothers. It made no difference that the babies could see, hear and smell their mothers; without touching, the babies became apathetic, and failed to progress.

E For humans, insufficient touching in early years can have lifelong results. 'In touching cultures, adult aggression is low, whereas in cultures where touch is limited, adult aggression is high,' writes Tiffany Field, director of the Touch Research Institutes at the University of Miami School of Medicine. Studies of a variety of cultures show a correspondence between high rates of physical affection in childhood and low rates of adult physical violence.

F While the effects of touching are easy to understand, the mechanics of it are less so. 'Your skin has millions of nerve cells of various shapes at different depths,' explains Stanley Bolanowski, a neuroscientist and associate director of the Institute for Sensory Research at Syracuse University. 'When the nerve cells are stimulated, physical energy is transformed into energy used by the nervous system and passed from the skin to the spinal cord and brain. It's called transduction, and no one knows exactly how it takes place.' Suffice it to say that the process involves the intricate, split-second operation of a complex system of signals between neurons in the skin and brain.

G This is starting to sound very confusing until Bolanowski says: 'In simple terms people perceive three basic things via skin: pressure, temperature, and pain.' And then I'm sure he's wrong. 'When I get wet, my skin feels wet,' I protest. 'Close your eyes and lean back,' says Bolanowski.

H Something cold and wet is on my forehead – so wet, in fact, that I wait for water to start dripping down my cheeks. 'Open your eyes.' Bolanowski says, showing me that the sensation comes from a chilled, but dry, metal cylinder. The combination of pressure and cold, he explains, is what makes my skin perceive wetness. He gives me a surgical glove to put on and has me put a finger in a glass of cold water. My finger feels wet, even though I have visual proof that it's not touching water. My skin, which seemed so reliable, has been deceiving me my entire life. When I shower or wash my hands, I now realize, my skin feels pressure and temperature. It's my brain that says I feel wet.

I Perceptions of pressure, temperature and pain manifest themselves in many different ways. Gentle stimulation of pressure receptors can result in ticklishness; gentle stimulation of pain receptors, in itching.

Both sensations arise from a neurological transmission, not from something that physically exists. Skin, I'm realizing, is under constant assault, both from within the body and from forces outside. Repairs occur with varying success.

J Take the spot where I nicked myself with a knife while slicing fruit. I have a crusty scab surrounded by pink tissue about a quarter inch long on my right palm. Under the scab, epidermal cells are migrating into the wound to close it up. When the process is complete, the scab will fall off to reveal new epidermis. It's only been a few days, but my little self-repair is almost complete. Likewise, we recover quickly from slight burns. If you ever happen to touch a hot burner, just put your finger in cold water. The chances are you will have no blister, little pain and no scar. Severe burns, though, are a different matter.

Questions 1–4

The passage has 10 paragraphs A–J.

Which paragraph contains the following information?

Write the correct letter A–J in boxes 1–4 on your answer sheet.

1   the features of human skin, on and below the surface

2   an experiment in which the writer can see what is happening

3   advice on how you can avoid damage to the skin

4   cruel research methods used in the past

Questions 5 and 6

Choose the correct letter, A, B, C or D.

Write your answres in boxes 5 and 6 on your answer sheet.

5   How does a lack of affectionate touching affect children?

    A   It makes them apathetic.

    B   They are more likely to become violent adults.

    C   They will be less aggressive when they grow up.

    D   We do not really know.

6   After the 'wetness' experiments, the writer says that

    A   his skin is not normal.

    B   his skin was wet when it felt wet.

    C   he knew why it felt wet when it was dry.

    D   the experiments taught him nothing new.

Questions 7–11

*Complete each sentence with the correct ending **A–I** from the box below.*

*Write the correct letter **A–I** in boxes 7–11 on your answer sheet.*

7   Touch is unique among the five senses

8   A substance may feel wet

9   Something may tickle

10   The skin may itch

11   A small cut heals up quickly

A   because it is both cold and painful.

B   because the outer layer of the skin can mend itself.

C   because it can be extremely thin.

D   because there is light pressure on the skin.

E   because we do not need the others to survive.

F   because there is a good blood supply to the skin.

G   because of a small amount of pain.

H   because there is a low temperature and pressure.

I   because it is hurting a lot.

J   because all humans are capable of experiencing it.

Questions 12–14

Do the following statements agree with the information given in Reading Passage 1?

In boxes 12–14 on your answer sheet write

> **TRUE**   *if the statement agrees with the information*
>
> **FALSE**   *if the statement contradicts the information*
>
> **NOT GIVEN**   *if there is no information on this*

12   Even scientists have difficulty understanding how our sense of touch works.

13   The skin is more sensitive to pressure than to temperature or pain.

14   The human skin is always good at repairing itself.

Reading passage 2

*You should spend about 20 minutes on **Questions 15–27**, which are based on Reading Passage 2.*

Questions 15–19

*Reading passage 2 has five sections **A–E**.*

*Choose the most suitable headings for sections **A–E** from the list of headings below.*

Write the correct number i–x in boxes 15–19 on your answer sheet.

List of headings

i	How to make the locks in your home more secure
ii	How to open a lock without a key
iii	Choosing the right tools to open locks
iv	The cylinder and the bolt
v	How to open a lock with a different key
vi	Lock varieties
vii	How a basic deadbolt system works
viii	The people who open locks without a key
ix	How a cylinder lock works
x	How to pick different kinds of lock

---

15 Section A

16 Section B

17 Section C

18 Section D

19 Section E

How Lock Picking Works

Section A

Lock picking is an essential skill for locksmiths because it lets them get past a lock without destroying it. When you lock yourself out of your house or lose your key, a locksmith can let you back in very easily.

Lock-picking skills are not particularly common among burglars, mainly because there are so many other, simpler ways of breaking into a house (throwing a brick through a back window, for example). For the most part, only intruders who need to cover their tracks, such as spies and detectives, will bother to pick a lock.

Simply understanding the principles of lock picking may change your whole attitude toward locks and keys. Lock picking clearly demonstrates that normal locks are not infallible devices. They provide a level of security that can be breached with minimal effort. With the right tools, a determined intruder can break into almost anything.

Section B

Locksmiths define lock-picking as the manipulation of a lock's components to open a lock without a key. To understand lock-picking, then, you first have to know how locks and keys work.

Think about the normal deadbolt lock you might find on a front door. In this sort of lock, a movable bolt or latch is embedded in the door so it can be extended out to the side. This bolt is lined up with a notch in the frame. When you turn the lock, the bolt extends into the notch in the frame, so the door can't move. When you retract the bolt, the door moves freely. The lock's only job is to make it simple for someone with a key to move the bolt but difficult for someone without a key to move it.

Section C

The most widely-used lock design is the cylinder lock. In this kind, the key turns a cylinder in the middle of the lock, which turns the attached mechanism. When the cylinder is turned one way, the mechanism pulls in on the bolt and the door can open. When the cylinder turns the other way, the mechanism releases the bolt so the door cannot open.

One of the most common cylinder locks is the pin design. Its main components are the housing (the outer part of the lock which does not move), the central cylinder, and several vertical shafts that run down from the housing into the cylinder. Inside these shafts are pairs of metal pins of varying length, held in position by small springs.

Without the key, the pins are partly in the housing and partly in the cylinder, so that the mechanism cannot turn and the lock, therefore, cannot open. When you put the correct key into the cylinder, the notches in the key push each pair of pins up just enough so that the top pin is completely in the housing and the bottom pin is entirely in the cylinder. It now turns freely, and you can open the lock.

Section D

To pick a pin lock, you simply move each pin pair into the correct position, one by one. There are two main tools used in the picking process.

Picks: long, thin pieces of metal that curve up at the end (like a dentist's pick).

A tension wrench: the simplest sort of tension wrench is a thin screwdriver.

The first step in picking a lock is to insert the tension wrench into the keyhole and turn it in the same direction that you would turn the key. This turns the cylinder so that it is slightly offset from the housing around it, creating a slight ledge in the pin shafts.

While applying pressure on the cylinder, you slide the pick into the keyhole and begin lifting the pins. The object is to lift each pin pair up to the level at which the top pin moves completely into the housing, as if pushed by the correct key.

When you do this while applying pressure with the tension wrench, you feel or hear a slight click when the pin falls into position. This is the sound of the upper pin falling into place on the ledge in the shaft. The ledge keeps the upper pin wedged in the housing, so it won't fall back down into the cylinder. In this way, you move each pin pair into the correct position until all the upper pins are pushed completely into the housing and all the lower pins rest inside the cylinder. At this point, the cylinder rotates freely and you can open the lock.

Section E
You'll find pin locks everywhere, from houses to padlocks. They are so popular because they are relatively inexpensive but offer moderate security.

Another common type of cylinder lock is the wafer lock. These work the same basic way as pin locks, but they have flat, thin pieces of metal called wafers rather than pins. You pick the wafers exactly the same way you pick pins – in fact, it is a little bit easier to pick wafer locks because the keyhole is wider. Despite giving relatively low security, these locks are found in most cars.

Tubular locks provide superior protection to pin and wafer locks, but they are also more expensive. Instead of one row of pins, tubular locks have pins positioned all the way around the circumference of the cylinder. This makes them much harder to pick. Conventional lock-picking techniques don't usually work on this type of lock, which is why they are often found on vending machines.

Questions 20–22

Complete the diagram below.

Choose NO MORE THAN THREE WORDS from the passage for each answer.

Write your answers in boxes 20–22 on your answer sheet.

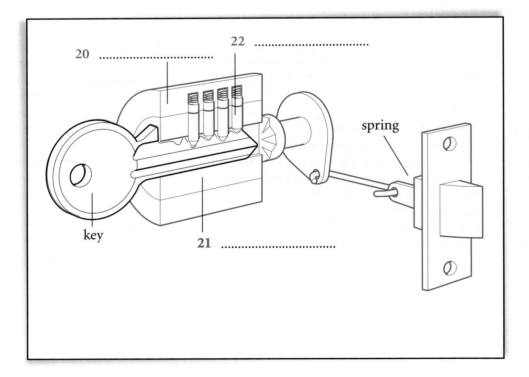

Questions 23–25

Complete the notes below.

Choose NO MORE THAN THREE WORDS from the passage for each answer.

Write your answers in boxes 23–25 on your answer sheet.

Picking a lock

Turn cylinder slightly using 23 ....

Hold cylinder still and insert 24 ....

Push top pin into shaft.

Hold top pin above cylinder, on 25 ....

Lift and hold all other pins in same way.

Turn cylinder and open lock.

Questions 26–27

Complete the table below.

Choose NO MORE THAN THREE WORDS from the passage for each answer.

Write your answers in boxes 26–27 on your answer sheet.

Type of lock	How secure?	Where used?
Pin	26	houses, padlocks, etc
27	relatively low security	most cars
Tubular	superior protection	vending machines

Reading passage 3

*You should spend about 20 minutes on **Questions 28–40**, which are based on Reading Passage 3.*

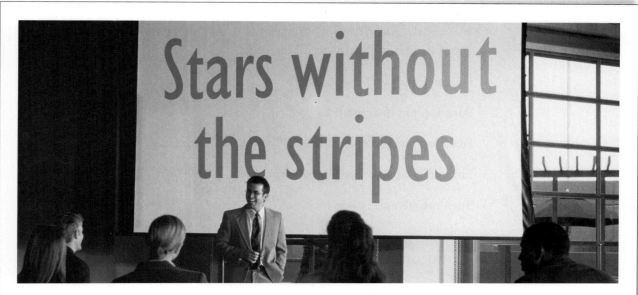

Managing cultural diversity is a core component of most masters programmes these days. The growth of Japanese corporations in the sixties and seventies reminded us that there were other models of business than those taught by Harvard professors and US-based management consultants. And the cultural limits to the American model have more recently been
10 underlined by developments in Russia and central Europe over the past decade.

Yet in Britain, we are still more ready to accept the American model of management than most other European countries. As a result, UK managers often fail to understand how business practices are fundamentally different on the Continent. One outcome is that many mergers and acquisitions, strategic alliances and joint ventures between British
20 and European companies do not achieve their objectives and end in tears.

Alternatively, managers may avoid a merger or joint venture which makes sense from a hard-nosed strategic point of view because they fear that different working practices will prevent their goals from being achieved.

Essentially, Anglo-Saxon companies are structured on the principles of project
30 management. In the eighties, companies were downsized, with tiers of management eliminated. In the nineties, management fashion embraced the ideas of business process re-engineering, so organizations were broken down into customer-focused trading units. Sometimes these were established as subsidiary companies, at other times as profit-and-loss or cost centres.

Over the past ten years, these principles
40 have been applied as vigorously to the UK public sector as to private-sector corporations. Hospitals, schools, universities, social services departments, as well as large areas of national government, now operate on project management principles – all with built-in operational targets, key success factors, and performance-related reward systems.

The underlying objectives for this
50 widespread process of organizational

restructuring have been to increase the transparency of operations, encourage personal accountability, become more efficient at delivering service to customer, and directly relate rewards to performance.

The result is a management culture which is entrepreneurially oriented and focused almost entirely on the short term, and highly segmented organizational structures – since employee incentives and rewards are geared to the activities of their own particular unit.

This business model has also required development of new personal skills. We are now encouraged to lead, rather than to manage by setting goals and incentive systems for staff. We have to be cooperative team members rather than work on our own. We have to accept that, in flattened and decentralized organizations, there are very limited career prospects. We are to be motivated by target-related rewards rather than a longer-term commitment to our employing organization.

This is in sharp contrast to the model of management that applies elsewhere in Europe. The principles of business process re-engineering have never been fully accepted in France, Germany and the other major economies; while in some Eastern European economies, the attempt to apply them in the nineties brought the economy virtually to its knees, and created huge opportunities for corrupt middle managers and organized crime.

Instead, continental European companies have stuck to the bureaucratic model which delivered economic growth for them throughout the twentieth century. European corporations continue to be structured hierarchically, with clearly defined job descriptions and explicit channels of reporting. Decision making, although incorporating consultative processes, remains essentially top-down.

Which of these two models is preferable? Certainly, the downside of the Anglo-American model is now becoming evident, not least in the long-hours working culture that the application of the decentralized project management model inevitably generates.

Whether in a hospital, a software start-up or a factory, the breakdown of work processes into project-driven targets leads to over-optimistic goals and underestimates of the resources needed. The result is that the success of projects often demands excessively long working hours if the targets are to be achieved.

Further, the success criteria, as calibrated in performance targets, are inevitably arbitrary, and the source of ongoing dispute. Witness the objections of teachers and medics to the performance measures applied to them by successive governments. This is not surprising. In a factory producing cars the output of individuals is directly measurable, but what criteria can be used to measure output and performance in knowledge-based activities such as R&D labs, government offices, and even the marketing departments of large corporations?

The demands and stresses of operating according to the Anglo-American model seem to be leading to increasing rates of personnel burn-out. It is not surprising that managers queue for early retirement. In a recent survey, just a fifth said they would work to 65. This could be why labour market participation rates have declined so dramatically for British 50-year-olds in the past twenty years.

By contrast, the European management model allows for family-friendly employment policies and working hours directives to be implemented. It encourages staff to have a long-term psychological commitment to their employing organizations. Of course, companies operating on target-focused project management principles may be committed to family-friendly employment policies in theory. But, if the business plan has to be finished by the end of the month, the advertising campaign completed by the end of next week, and patients pushed through the system to achieve measurable targets, are we really going to let down our 'team' by clocking out at 5 p.m. and taking our full entitlement of annual leave?

Perhaps this is why we admire the French for their quality of life.

Questions 28–31

Do the following statements agree with the writer's views in Reading Passage 3?

In boxes 28–31 on your answer sheet write

> **YES**   *if the statement agrees with the views of the writer*
>
> **NO**   *if the statement does not agree with the views of the writer*
>
> **NOT GIVEN**   *if there is no information about this in the passage*

28   Attempts by British and mainland European firms to work together often fail.

29   Project management principles discourage consideration of long-term issues.

30   There are good opportunities for promotion within segmented companies.

31   The European model gives more freedom of action to junior managers.

Questions 32–37

Complete the summary below.

Choose the answers from the box and write the corresponding words in boxes 32–37 on your answer sheet. There are more choices than spaces, so you will not need to use all of them.

Adopting the US model in Britain has had negative effects. These include the 32 .... hours spent at work, as small sections of large organizations struggle to 33 .... unrealistic short-term objectives. Nor is there 34 .... on how to calculate the productivity of professional, technical, and clerical staff, who cannot be assessed in the same way as 35 .... employees. In addition, managers within this culture are finding the 36 .... of work too great, with 80% reported to be 37 .... to carry on working until the normal retirement age.

List of words

argument	temperature	reach	manufacturing
increasing	able	office	pressure
negative	predict	declining	agreement
discussion	no	willing	unwilling

Questions 38–39

Complete the notes below.

Choose NO MORE THAN THREE WORDS from Reading Passage 3 for each answer.

Write your answers in boxes 38–39 on your answer sheet.

38 Working conditions in mainland Europe are in practice more likely to be

....

39 UK managers working to tight deadlines probably give up some of their

....

Question 40

Choose the correct letter A, B, C or D. Write your answer in box 40 on your answer sheet.

Which of the following statements best describes the writer's main purpose in Reading Passage 3?

A   to argue that Britain should have adopted the Japanese model of management many years ago

B   to criticize Britain's adoption of the US model, as compared to the European model.

C   to propose a completely new model that would be neither American nor European

D   to point out the negative effects of the existing model on the management of hospitals in Britain

Academic Writing   1 hour

The writing test consists of two tasks. You should attempt both tasks.

Writing Task 1

You should spend about 20 minutes on this task.

The charts below show the number of girls per 100 boys in all levels of education.

Summarize the information by selecting and reporting on the main features, and make comparisons where relevant.

Write at least 150 words.

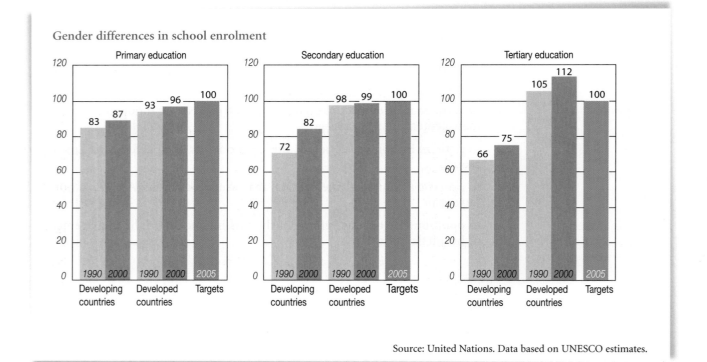

Gender differences in school enrolment

Source: United Nations. Data based on UNESCO estimates.

Question Strategies: reporting bar graphs and making comparisons

If there is more than one diagram, study any heading, key or source for each.

Decide what the vertical and horizontal axes measure, and what the bars show.

Look for similarities, differences, changes and trends.

Make comparisons both within and between diagrams. Describe similarities, e.g. *There was almost the same rise in … as in …* , and differences, e.g. *The main difference between … and … was that … .*

Composition Strategies: writing task 1

You only have 20 minutes to do Writing Task 1, so make sure the points you include are:

• **relevant** – you will waste time and lose marks if you don't follow the instructions. Don't speculate or add your own opinions.

• **not repetitive** – don't say the same thing in different words, or write similar sentences about all the figures. Describe something different in every point. Make comparisons and describe trends rather than focus on individual numbers.

• **accurate** – giving the wrong information loses marks, so study the question carefully and interpret data or diagrams correctly.

Improve your skills: making comparisons

Which of these do we use to talk about similarities, and which for differences?

1 Compared to … , the change in … was dramatic.
2 The … weren't so close to their target as the … were.
3 In … , the gap narrowed. In the same way, …
4 The percentage of … in … dropped much faster than in … .
5 In both … and … , the proportion of … was growing.
6 The number of … declined as rapidly in … as in … .
7 While the … went up substantially, the … increased slowly.
8 In neither … nor … was there any significant fall.
9 The total number of … in … shot up, as did those in … .
10 The figures for … showed a … per cent rise, whereas those for … fell by … per cent.

▶ Check your answers on page 97 before you continue

Improve your skills: points to include

Which of these points are suitable for the task above? Cross out the points you would not use, writing *irrelevant*, *repetitive* or *inaccurate* next to each.

a In developed countries, there was a higher proportion of girls at all levels than in developing countries.
b The figures for girls and boys in secondary schools are similar in my country.
c From 1990 to 2000, there was a much bigger increase in female enrolments in developed countries than in developing countries.
d By 2000, females in tertiary education in developed countries outnumbered males.
e At primary, secondary and tertiary levels, there were fewer girls per 100 boys in developing countries than in developed ones.
f Secondary schools in developing countries will probably not meet their target until about 2020.

▶ Check your answers on page 97 before you continue

Writing task 2

You should spend about 40 minutes on this task.

Write about the following topic:

Directors of large companies often receive much bigger salary increases than ordinary workers. Employers' organizations say that in a global market this is necessary to attract the best management talent.

What are your views?

Give reasons for your answer and include any relevant examples from your own knowledge and experience.

Write at least 250 words.

Improve your skills: using appropriate language

Decide which of these pairs is usually more appropriate for IELTS writing. Explain why in each case.

1 a   There isn't any proof.
  b   There is no proof.

2 a   These are dangerous people.
  b   These are dangerous guys.

3 a   The authorities should not tolerate this.
  b   The authorities should not put up with this.

4 a   It must be done asap.
  b   It must be done as soon as possible.

5 a   Therefore, I disagree with the statement.
  b   So I disagree with the statement.

6 a   'Don't buy it,' safety experts told the public.
  b   Safety experts advised the public not to buy it.

7 a   It is alleged that he committed a crime.
  b   People allege that he committed a crime.

8 a   It is a question which there is no simple answer to.
  b   It is a question to which there is no simple answer.

9 a   The latest figures are even worse. They came out yesterday.
  b   The latest figures, which came out yesterday, are even worse.

Can you think of any other features of informal speech to avoid in IELTS writing?

▶ Check your answers on page 97 before you continue.

Speaking

Part 1

You will be asked some general questions about a range of familair topic area. This part lasts between four and five minutes.

What is your full name?

What do people usually call you?

Where are you from?

Your school days.

What do you remember about your first school, when you were a child?

In what ways did life at school change as you became older?

What was your favourite subject? Why?

Going abroad.

What experience do you have of travelling to other countries?

Which country would you especially like to visit? Why?

What are the best ways to get to know a country?

What are the biggest cultural differences between your country and English-speaking countries?

Different kinds of entertainment.

What sort of television programmes do you like watching?

How has television in your country changed in recent years?

Which do you prefer: the cinema, the theatre, or live music? Why?

Tell me about a popular form of public entertainment in your country.

Part 2

You will be given a topic to talk about for one to two minutes. Before you talk, you will have one minute to think about what you are going to say. You will be given paper and a pencil to make notes if you wish. Here is the topic:

Describe a place that has a special meaning to you.
You should say:
    what kind of place it is and where it is
    what it looks like
    what sounds you associate with it
    and explain why you particularly like the place.

Follow-up questions:

When do you think you will next go there?

How would you feel if the place changed in a significant way?

Part 3

You will be asked some questions about abstract issues and concepts related to the topic in Part 2. This discussion lasts between four and five minutes.

Leaving the family home

Why do many people leave home when they are still quite young?

What personal qualities do you feel are required for a young person to live on their own?

Moving from place to place

In many countries there has been large-scale migration from the countryside to the cities. Do you think this is positive or negative?

Do you think that the possibility of working from home via the Internet will lead to many people going back to the countryside?

Growing cities

In what ways do the new megacities of Asia, Africa, and South America differ from older ones such as London or New York?

Should there be a limit on the size of cities?

Improve your skills key

Academic Writing

Making comparisons page 93
Similarities: 3, 5, 6, 8, 9.
Differences: 1, 2, 4, 7, 10.

Points to include page 93
a   include
b   *irrelevant*
c   *inaccurate*
d   include
e   *repetitive* (same as (a))
f   *irrelevant*

Using appropriate language page 94
1b avoid contracted form
2a avoid colloquial word
3a single-word verb preferred to phrasal verb
4b avoid abbreviation or acronym
5a formal linker preferred
6b reported speech rather than direct speech
7a passive preferred to active.
8b avoid ending with preposition
9b complex sentence (here, a relative clause) rather
    than simple sentences
Other features of informal speech: exclamation
marks, slang, omitted pronouns, etc.

Test 4

Listening 30 minutes

Section 1

Questions 1–4

Answer the questions below.

Write NO MORE THAN THREE WORDS for each answer.

Which documents could Sam use as proof of her name?

Example   passport

1 ....

2 ....

Which could she use as proof of her address?

council tax bill

3 ....

phone bill (fixed line)

4 ....

Questions 5–7

Complete the notes below.

Write NO MORE THAN TWO WORDS OR NUMBERS for each answer.

Name of bank?	Savings Bank
Open which days?	Monday–Friday
Opening hours?	5 ....
Where?	6 ....
Free gift?	7 ....

Questions 8–10

*Match the places in Questions 8–10 to the appropriate letters **A–H** on the map.*

8   Royal Bank .... F

9   Northern Bank .... A

10   National Bank C

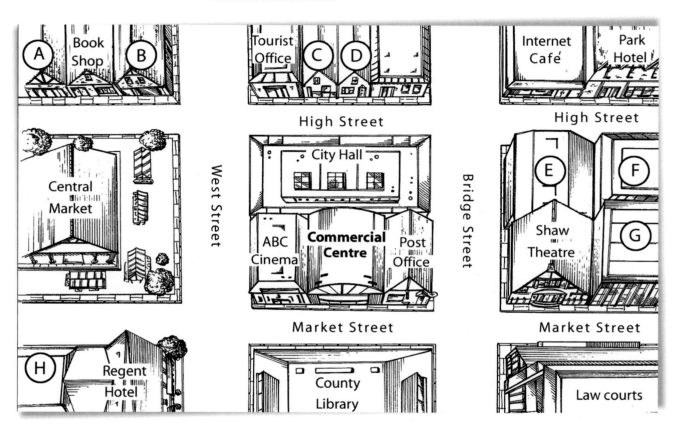

Section 2

Questions 11–14

Complete the table below.

Write NO MORE THAN THREE WORDS for each answer.

Preparing for the interview

What to do	How to do it
Step 1: **Prepare things to take.**	Gather all documents, e.g. copies of résumé. Choose 11 ...~~work samples~~... , e.g. designs, drawings, written work.
Step 2: **Get more information.**	Check you have pen and paper. Ask firm for a 12 ...*post*... . See profiles at Chamber of Commerce, library.
Step 3: **Focus on you and the job.**	Contact 13 ...*company*... of this or related firms. Compare yourself with what is required. Imagine likely questions and your answers. Decide how to make up for any 14 ...*experie*... you lack.

Questions 15–20

Complete the notes below.

Write NO MORE THAN THREE WORDS for each answer.

At the interview

Arrive no more than 15 ...*10 minutes*... before the time of the interview.

After you hear the question, you can 16 .... before you reply.

You can 17 *ask for clarification* if you don't understand what they're asking you.

Wait for them to offer you the job before you say what 18 .... you want.

Learning from the experience will make you more 19 ...*confidence*... in future interviews.

Pay attention to your 20 ...*apperence*... – it shows you have a positive attitude.

Section 3

Questions 21–24

Complete the summary below by writing NO MORE THAN THREE WORDS in the spaces provided.

To many employers, academic success and personal development as a result of being at 21 ..Select..modules.... can be as important as course content, so choose 22 .... modules that you may do well in. You should, however, think more carefully about your choice if your course is 23 ....Crusial........... . In this case the course normally includes all the modules necessary for professional training, but if you are in any doubt check with your academic department or the 24 .... at the university.

Questions 25–29

*Write the appropriate letters **A–C** against questions 25–29.*

Which modules have the following features?

    A   Applied Chemical Engineering

    B   Fluid Mechanics

    C   Chemical Engineering: Science 1

25 developing computer skills ....A...

26 exemption from part of a module ....C....

27 assessment by formal examination ....B....

28 developing speaking and writing skills .....A......

29 learning through problem solving ......C.....

Question 30

30 Which chart shows the percentage of private study time on the Spanish 1A module?

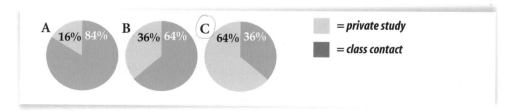

Section 4

Questions 31–33

Label the diagram. Write NO MORE THAN TWO WORDS AND/OR A NUMBER for each answer.

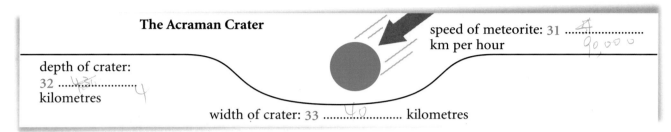

The Acraman Crater

speed of meteorite: 31 .... km per hour

depth of crater: 32 .... kilometres

width of crater: 33 .... kilometres

Questions 34–36

*Choose from letters **A–C** and write them on your answer sheet.*

34 The crater at Acraman is

    A   nowadays entirely covered by sea water.

    B   one of the most beautiful on Earth.

    C   less spectacular than others in Australia.

35 Williams realized what had happened at Acraman when he

    A   saw pictures of the area taken from above.

    B   visited Acraman for the first time in 1980.

    C   noticed a picture of the crater in a textbook.

36 Where was rock from Acraman found?

    A   Only in the Flinders mountains.

    B   At several places over 300 km from Acraman.

    C   At a place 500 km from Acraman, but nowhere else.

Questions 37–40

Write NO MORE THAN THREE WORDS for each answer.

37 What made the sea water shake? ....

38 What threw the pebbles into the air? ....

39 What was mixed with silt to form a layer of rock? ....

40 What shaped the ripples on top of the rock? ....

Academic Reading 1 hour

Reading passage 1

*You should spend about 20 minutes on **Questions 1–13**, which are based on Reading Passage 1.*

The Power of Light

Light reveals the world to us. It sets our biological clocks. It triggers in our brains the sensations of colour. Light feeds us, supplying the energy for plants to grow. It inspires us with special effects like rainbows and sunsets. Light gives us life-changing tools, from incandescent bulbs to lasers and fibre optics.

There has been light from the beginning. There will be light, feebly, at the end. In all its
10 forms, visible and invisible, it saturates the universe. Light is more than a little bit inscrutable. Modern physics has sliced the stuff of nature into ever smaller and more exotic constituents, but light won't reduce. Light is light – pure, but not simple. No one is quite sure how to describe it. A wave? A particle? Yes, the scientists say. Both.

It is a measure of light's importance in our daily lives that we hardly pay any attention to
20 it. Light is almost like air. It's a given. A human would no more linger over the concept of light than a fish would ponder the notion of water. There are exceptions, certain moments of sudden appreciation when a particular manifestation of light, a transitory glory, appears: a rainbow, a sunset, a flash of lightning in a dark sky, the shimmering surface of the sea at twilight, the dappled light in a forest, the little red dot from a professor's laser
30 pointer. The flicker of a candle, flooding a room with romance. The torch searching for the circuit breakers after a power cut.

Usually, though, we don't see light, we merely see with it. You can't appreciate the beauty of a rose if you ponder that the colour red is just the brain's interpretation of a specific wavelength of light with crests that are roughly 700 nanometres apart. A theatrical lighting director told me that she's doing her
40 job best when no one notices the lights at all. Her goal is to create an atmosphere, a mood - not to show off the fancy new filters that create colours of startling intensity.

Light is now used for everything from laser eye surgery to telephone technology. It could even become the main power source for long-distance space travel. The spaceship would have an ultrathin sail to catch the 'wind' of light beamed from an Earth-based laser. In theory such a craft could accelerate to a sizeable fraction of the speed of light, without carrying fuel.

What we call light is really the same thing in a different set of wavelengths as the radiation that we call radio waves or gamma rays or x-rays. But visible light is unlike any other fundamental element of the universe: it directly, regularly and dramatically interacts with our senses. Light offers high-resolution information across great distances. You can't hear or smell the moons of Jupiter or the Crab Nebula. So much of vital importance is communicated by visible light that almost everything from a fly to an octopus has a way to capture it – an eye, eyes, or something similar.

It's worth noting that our eyes are designed to detect the kind of light that is radiated in abundance by the particular star that gives life to our planet: the sun. Visible light is powerful stuff, moving at relatively short wavelengths, which makes it biologically convenient. To see long, stretched-out radio waves, we'd have to have huge eyes like satellite dishes. Not worth the trouble! Nor would it make sense for our eyes to detect infrared light (though some deep-sea shrimp near hot springs do see this way). We'd be constantly distracted, because in these wavelengths any heat-emitting object glows. That would include almost everything around us.

There is also darkness in the daytime: shadows. There are many kinds of shadows, more than I realized until I consulted astronomer and shadow expert David Lynch in Topanga Canyon, up the coast from Santa Monica, California. Lynch points out that a shadow is filled with light reflected from the sky, otherwise it would be completely black. Black is the way shadows on the moon looked to the Apollo astronauts, because the moon has no atmosphere and thus no sky to bounce light into the unlit crannies of the lunar surface.

Lynch is a man who, when he looks at a rainbow, spots details that elude most of us. He knows, for example, that all rainbows come in pairs, and he always looks for the second rainbow: a faint, parallel rainbow, with the colours in reverse order. The intervening region is darker. That area has a name, wouldn't you know: Alexander's dark band. As I took in the spectacular view across the canyon, Lynch explained something else: 'the reason those mountains over there look a little blue,' he said, indicating the range that obscures the Pacific, 'is because there's sky between here and those mountains. It's called airlight.'

What next for light? What new application will we see? What orthodoxy-busting cosmic information will starlight deliver to our telescopes? Will the rotating disco ball ever make a dance-floor comeback? Above all, you have to wonder: will we ever fully understand light?

There have been recent headlines about scientists finding ways to make light go faster than the speed of light. This is what science fiction writers and certain overly imaginative folks have dreamed of for decades. If you could make a spaceship that wasn't bound by Einstein's speed limit, they fantasized, you could zip around the universe far more easily.

Lijun Wang, a research scientist at Princeton, managed to create a pulse of light that went faster than the supposed speed limit. 'We created an artificial medium of cesium gas in which the speed of a pulse of light exceeds the speed of light in a vacuum,' he said, 'but this is not at odds with Einstein.' Even though light can be manipulated to go faster than light, matter can't. Information can't. There's no possibility of time travel.

I asked Wang why light goes 186,282 miles a second and not some other speed. 'That's just the way nature is,' he said. There are scientists who don't like 'why' questions like this. The speed of light is just what it is. That's their belief. Whether light would move at a different velocity in a different universe is something that is currently outside the scope of experimental science. It's even a bit 'out there' for the theorists.

What's certain is that light is going to remain extremely useful for industry, science, art, and our daily, mundane comings and goings. Light permeates our reality at every scale of existence. It's an amazing tool, a carrier of beauty, a giver of life. I can't help but say that it has a very bright future.

Questions 1–5

Reading passage 3 describes a number of cause and effect relationships. Match each Cause (1–5) in List A, with its Effect (A–H) in List B.

Write your answers (A–H) in boxes 1–5 on your answer sheet.

There are more Effects in List B than you will need, so you will not use all of them.

List A Causes

1 Much of the time, visible light is all around us.

2 Light can sometimes appear in an interesting way.

3 Visible light carries a lot of essential information.

4 Without an atmosphere, light is not reflected onto solid surfaces.

5 Only light can exceed 186,282 miles per second.

List B Effects

A Nearly all living creatures can detect it.

B There is a dark gap between rainbows.

C Light from Earth could power a spacecraft.

D Shadows are totally black.

E We cannot return to the past.

F We don't really notice or think about it.

G Certain creatures can detect infra-red light.

H We instantly become aware of it.

Questions 6–10

Do the following statements agree with the views of the writer in Reading Passage 1?

In boxes 6–10 on your answer sheet write

> **YES**   *if the statement agrees with the views of the writer*
>
> **NO**   *if the statement does not agree with the views of the writer*
>
> **NOT GIVEN**   *if there is no information about this in the passage*

6   It is difficult to find a single word to say exactly what light is.

7   Thinking about the physics of light can make an object seem even more beautiful.

8   Light from the sun makes it possible for life to exist on other planets.

9   It is more practical for humans to detect visible light rather than radio waves.

10   David Lynch sometimes notices things that other people don't.

Questions 11–13

Answer the following questions using NO MORE THAN THREE WORDS for each answer.

Write your answers in boxes 11-13 on your answer sheet.

11   What appearance can the land have when seen from a distance?

....

12   In what have some people imagined travelling? ....

13   In what substance did light go faster than previously thought possible?

....

Reading passage 2

*You should spend about 20 minutes on **Questions 14–27**, which are based on Reading Passage 2.*

To MBA or not to MBA?

'You could be forgiven for thinking just about every man and his dog has an MBA these days,' says Anthony Hesketh, of Lancaster University management school. We know what he means. Such is the worldwide growth and awareness of the MBA that this icon of career advancement and high salaries has almost become synonymous with postgraduate education in the business sector.

In reality, many postgraduate alternatives to an
10 MBA exist. The total number of MBA programmes worldwide is around 2,400, while other masters and advanced courses in the whole spectrum of business education add up to more than 10,000.

Two key distinctions exist in matching what aspiring students want with what the universities offer: first is generalization versus specialization, and second is pre-experience versus post-experience, and the two distinctions are interlinked. Carol Blackman, of the University of
20 Westminster school of business, explains the first distinction. 'Specialist masters programmes are designed either for career preparation in a clearly defined type of job or profession, or are intended to develop or enhance professional competence in individuals who are already experienced. The aim is to increase the depth of their knowledge in the specialist area. The MBA, on the other hand, is a general management programme which provides practising managers with an opportunity for
30 personal development with a broadly-based introduction to all management subject areas and the theory and practice of management'.

Specialist knowledge, however, is not everything when it comes to finding a job. Surveys by the UK's Association of Graduate Recruiters (AGR) repeatedly confirm that what employers seek, and continue to find scarce, are the personal skills that will make graduates valuable employees. In fact, when recruiting new graduates, most employers considered these skills more important than specialist knowledge. What employers seek most from new graduates are enthusiasm and self-motivation, interpersonal skills, team working and good oral communication. Of the nineteen skills considered important in AGR's 2002 survey, just three require specialist education – numeracy, computer literacy and foreign languages – and these are low on the list.

Nunzio Quacquarelli, chief executive of topcareers.net, takes this further. 'Clearly, salary differentials for those with a second degree, but no significant work experience, do not match those of a good MBA and a number of years in the workplace. According to the AGR research, about 14% of employers offered a better salary to those new graduates with a masters – or even a doctorate. In my view, the salary improvement of 10% to 15% largely reflects the recruit's age and earning expectancy rather than the increase in human capital perceived by the employer. Contrast this with our latest topmba.com MBA Recruiters Survey results which shows that the average salary paid to an MBA with good work experience in the US and Europe is US$80,000 – around two and a half times the average starting salary for a young postgraduate.'

Anthony Hesketh poses the question whether holding a second degree may even be a disadvantage. 'I have seen many reports over the years suggesting that employers view postgraduates as eminently less employable than those with a first degree. Drive, motivation and career focus, not to mention ability, are what employers value and are prepared to pay for. A postgraduate immediately has an uphill task explaining an additional year, or three years, of study.'

This view may seem cynical, but, if you are about to graduate and are considering a further degree, you should take the realities into account and ask yourself some hard questions:

- Is the qualification I am considering going to impress employers?
- Is it going to give me the edge over less qualified candidates?
- Is my consideration of a second degree because I am not sure of my career direction?

- Will employers consider that I lack drive and ambition because I have deferred my attempts to find a worthwhile job?

Many postgraduate options exist that can help you to acquire the personal skills that employers in the world of business are seeking. Consider, for example, the offerings of Strathclyde and Durham universities.

According to Dr Nic Beech, of the University of Strathclyde graduate school of business: 'The MSc in business management (MBM), offered at USGSB is suitable for students with a good first degree – particularly a non-business first degree – but little or no business experience. Our MBM offers these graduates the opportunity to combine the specialization of their first degree with a general management qualification – something employers recognize produces a well-rounded individual.

Graduates tell us that the MBM allows them to access sectors previously out of reach. It is designed to develop the business knowledge, practical experience and personal skills which employers are seeking.'

At the University of Durham business school, Sheena Maberly is careers development officer; she too sees high value in qualifications such as the Durham MA in management (DMAM). She says: 'Whatever your first degree, from anthropology to zoology, a postgraduate business degree can help you gain a competitive edge in an over-crowded job market. If you're just starting out in your career, a business masters degree like the DMAM will enable you to develop skills directly relevant to employers' needs. So, extending your studies into management can make you better equipped to 'hit the ground running' – and that's what employers expect. Recruiters are highly selective and a vocational qualification is additional evidence of motivation.'

Before committing yourself to postgraduate study, weigh up the options. Perhaps the best route might be to take a job now and plan to do an MBA a few years down the line? Try to get sponsorship from a company. Or go for a well researched and thoroughly thought through masters that will help you land a good job. Ultimately the choice is yours, but focus on the future, and on your target employer's expectations.

Questions 14–16

Do the following statements agree with the information given in Reading Passage 2?

In boxes 14–16 on your answer sheet write

TRUE	*if the statement agrees with the information*
FALSE	*if the statement contradicts the information*
NOT GIVEN	*if there is no information on this*

14   British employers are more interested in what potential recruits can do than what they know.

15   A recruit with a specialist masters usually earns as much as an experienced employee with a good MBA.

16   The writer claims that undergraduates often plan to do a masters because they can't decide what career to follow.

Questions 17–21

The text quotes various individuals. Match the four people A–D with the four points made in Questions 17–21. You may use any of the people more than once.

Write the appropriate letter (A–D) in boxes 17–21 on your answer sheet.

17   Employees with postgraduate qualifications earn more because they are older and expect more.

18   It can be difficult to convince an employer that the extra time spent at university was necessary.

19   One type of course focuses on a particular aspect of business, whereas the other is more general in approach.

20   Graduates who have neither worked in nor studied business are suited to our programme.

21   There is evidence that companies may prefer to employ people without a masters degree.

> **List of people**
> A Anthony Hesketh
> B Carol Blackman
> C Nunzio Quacquarelli
> D Nic Beech

Questions 22–27

Complete the summary below. Choose ONE word from Reading Passage 2 for each answer.

Write your answers in boxes 22–27 on your answer sheet.

According to Sheena Maberly, a second degree can improve the

22 .... prospects of graduates in any subject. Taking a

management MA gives them the 23 .... companies are looking

for, and lets them get straight on with the job as soon as they start work. It also

shows they have the 24 .... that companies seek.

First, however, it is important to consider the 25 ....: whether to

start right away on a carefully chosen postgraduate course, or to do so after a

few years' work, preferably with financial assistance from the

26 .... Whichever they decide, they should think about the

27 ...., and what the company wants.

Reading passage 3

*You should spend about 20 minutes on **Questions 28–40**, which are based on Reading Passage 3.*

Questions 28–33

*Reading passage 3 has seven paragraphs **A–G**.*

*Choose the most suitable headings for paragraphs **B–G** from the list of headings below.*

*Write the correct number **i–x** in boxes 28–33 on your answer sheet.*

List of headings
i   Looking at a particular decade
ii   Studying trees frozen in ice
iii   Bringing different studies together
iv   Records of different species compared
v   What dendrochronology is
vi   A war that affected the climate
vii   Showing how trees record volcanic activity
viii   A unique record of other times and places
ix   Local records covering thousands of years
x   How tree rings are formed

Example   Paragraph **A**   *Answer*   **v**

28   Paragraph **B**

29   Paragraph **C**

30   Paragraph **D**

31   Paragraph **E**

32   Paragraph **F**

33   Paragraph **G**

The Ring Cycle

A

In the jungle of scientific debate, you cannot always see the wood for the trees. But in climate change, the wood itself sometimes holds the key. Imagine an annual register of a year's sunshine and rainfall and frost, kept up to date with perfect accuracy almost everywhere south of the tundra and north of the tropics, and available for inspection not just at any time in life but, quite often, for centuries after death. The register is, of course, the annual growth rings of trees. Match the rings from young trees with those from old forest giants and you have a centuries-long measure of the march of the seasons. Match the rings from old trees with old cathedral rafters and you have a still longer chronology – and a science called dendrochronology.

B

Dendrochronologists, scientists who study the growth of rings in trees, have successfully constructed long tree-ring records by overlapping the patterns of wide and narrow rings in successively older timber specimens. There are now a dozen or so chronologies in the world that date back more than 5,000 years. These records, normally constructed in a restricted area, using a single species of tree, are year-by-year records of how the trees reacted to their growth conditions – an environmental history from the trees' point of view.

C

Because tree-ring chronologies are constructed on a regional basis, there has, in the past, been a tendency for dendrochronologists to think local. However, the success of dendrochronology as an international research topic means that there are now quite a lot of chronologies available for study. As the chronologies are dated absolutely, it is possible to compare the records from different areas year by year. Recently, an analysis of 383 modern chronologies, drawn from a vast area across Europe, northern Eurasia and North America was published. The authors, Keith Briffa and colleagues, observed that the maximum late-wood density of the growth rings in each year was related to the temperature in the growing season. Their analysis spanned 600 years, back to AD 1400, and presented a summer temperature record reconstructed from the huge grid of precisely dated ring densities. What they noticed was that the years of really low density – the cool summers – were directly associated with large explosive eruptions, as known from historical sources and from dated layers of acid in the Greenland ice record. Greenland ice is kilometres thick and is made up of the compressed snowfall of tens of thousands of years, so the ice record can be read in almost the same way as tree-rings. I shall use this study as an example of what else tree-rings can tell us.

D

The study provides a year-by-year estimate of temperatures, together with the dates of some major volcanoes. It is a nice clean story – volcanoes load the atmosphere with dust and aerosol and reflect back sunlight, cooling the earth's surface. This cooling leads to variations in the density of growth rings in northern conifers. Because there are a lot of other records, it is possible to test the findings from the conifer density record.

E

We can, for example, look at what European oak was doing across the same 600-year period. Was oak responding in the same way as the conifers? The 'oak chronology' is the mean of eight regional oak chronologies across a strip of land from Ireland to Poland. It represents how, on average, hundreds of millions of oaks grew. What we see from this comparison is that the oaks clearly do respond to the volcanoes in some cases (in 1602, 1740 and 1816, for instance), but nothing like so clearly in others. Immediately it becomes apparent that the conifers tell only part of the story. There are many downturns in oak growth, and only a few are related to the conifer record. The oaks were quite capable of being more stressed in years where the conifers were not affected. The point of this, however, is not to argue about the quality of global cooling; the point is to show what dendrochronology can do.

F

Take the case of 1816, called the 'year without a summer' because of the terrible unseasonable cold and the crop failures that ensued. It has long been known that the primary cause of the cooling was the massive eruption of Tambora, east of Java, in 1815. However, there was a lot more going on in the run-up to 1816. Bald cypress trees in Tennessee show a major growth anomaly, with rings up to 400 per cent wider than normal, in the years following a huge earthquake in 1811–12 in Eastern

America. But there is a volcanic acid layer in several Greenland and Antarctic ice cores in 1809–10, as well as in 1815–16. So here we have a combination of a highly unusual quake in an area of the USA not normally affected by earthquakes, and at least two volcanic eruptions, including Tambora, which is widely regarded as the largest in the last 10,000 years. According to Briffa, the period 1810–20 was the coldest in the last millennium, so we begin to see a combination of three unusual elements in less than ten years – exceptional earthquake, exceptional volcanic eruption, and exceptional cold. Given that the defeat of Napoleon's invasion of Russia in 1812 was famously attributed to 'General Winter', one wonders whether a natural series of events actually helped to change the course of modern history.

G

Obviously, the case of 1816 and the years just before and after it is relatively recent and well documented. However, dendrochronology allows us to investigate the effects of such events geographically, indeed globally. We can interrogate the trees in areas where there is no historical or instrumental record. Further back in time, dendrochronology is almost the only way to reconstruct abrupt environmental events and perhaps throw new light on far darker moments in human history. Were there just political forces at work in the Dark Ages, or did violent natural events also take a hand, tipping the balance by darkening the skies and lowering the temperature? The trees were there too, and kept a record. The wood hewn from them and preserved through the centuries is slowly beginning to yield at least circumstantial evidence that could support some of the stories – think of the Arthurian wasteland, or the plagues of Egypt – so far told only in enigmatic artefacts, or in legends, epics, and religious chronicles.

Questions 34–36

Which THREE of the following, are features of dendrochronology?

Write the appropriate letters A–F in boxes 34–36 on your answer sheet.

A   It provides a complete record of the weather in any part of the world.

B   It involves the study of ring patterns in trees of different ages.

C   A piece of wood cut a long time ago can form part of the record.

D   Studies show that trees of the same type all have the same number of rings.

E   As a science it has existed for over 5,000 years.

F   The oldest records are mostly of one type of tree in one place.

Questions 37–40

Choose the correct letters A, B, C or D. Write your answers in boxes 37–40 on your answer sheet.

37   What was the result of extending the research to the European oak?

    A   It added information to that obtained from studying conifers.

    B   It contradicted all the findings from the study of conifers.

    C   It showed exactly the same results as those for conifers.

    D   It proved that the world has cooled considerably since 1400 AD.

38   Which of these happened as a result of the eruption at Tambora?

    A   Agricultural production fell significantly.

    B   There was an earthquake in North America.

    C   Part of the polar ice caps melted.

    D   The outcome of a war changed.

39   By studying tree rings, we may discover

    A   whole new areas of human history.

    B   proof of events said to have happened.

    C   how earlier civilizations treated the environment.

    D   the truth about the nature of religious belief.

40   A suitable title for this passage would be

    A   How volcanoes and earthquakes changed history

    B   The influence of trees on the world's climate

    C   The role of trees in human history

    D   How trees can tell us more about the past

Academic Writing   1 hour

The writing test consists of two tasks. You should attempt both tasks.

Writing Task 1

You should spend about 20 minutes on this task.

The table below shows causes of injuries in Australia for teenagers and the general population.

Summarize the information by selecting and reporting the main features, making comparisons where relevant.

Write at least 150 words.

Teenagers and the total population: rates of certain injuries				
	Males aged 13–19	Females aged 13–19	Total aged 13–19	Total population
Cause	**rate**(a)	**rate**(a)	**rate**(a)	**rate**(a)
Total transport accidents	779	323	557	305
Car occupant	232	186	210	124
Motorcyclist	230	20	127	59
Pedal cyclist	210	24	120	45
Pedestrian	46	26	36	30
Falls	720	193	463	843
Complications of medical care	340	349	344	1431
Assault	281	80	183	119
Accidental poisoning	68	95	82	85
Exposure to heat, smoke, fire	54	17	36	42
All cases (b)	3688	1765	2750	3712

(a) Cases per 100,000 of this group.

(b) All cases, includes causes not listed. Some cases can involve more than one cause.

Writing Task 2

You should spend about 40 minutes on this task.

Write about the following topic:

Students should pay the full cost of their own university studies, rather than have free higher education provided by the state.

To what extent do you agree or disagree with this opinion?

Give reasons for your answer and include any relevant examples from your own knowledge or experience.

Write at least 250 words.

Speaking

Part 1

You will be asked some general questions about a range of familiar topic areas.
This part lasts between four and five minutes.

What is your full name?

What do people usually call you?

Where are you from?

Language learning.

What are your earliest memories of learning English?

What do find difficult about English?

What do you enjoy about learning it?

Which other languages have you studied?

Visitors to your country.

What are the main tourist attractions there?

What else would you recommend to foreign visitors?

Does/Would mass tourism benefit your country? Why?/Why not?

Communicating: by post, phone, email, text message, etc.

How do you keep in touch with your family and friends?

Tell me about an important message you have received.

How have mobile phones changed the way people communicate?

Part 2

You will be given a topic to talk about for one to two minutes. Before you talk, you will have one minute to think about what you are going to say. You will be given paper and a pencil to make notes if you wish. Here is the topic:

> Describe a present which you very much enjoyed receiving.
> You should say:
>   what is was
>   who gave it to you
>   what the occasion was
>   and explain why you were so pleased to receive it.

Follow-up questions:

Which do you enjoy more: giving or receiving presents?

Do you like presents to be a surprise, or do you prefer to choose what you are
    given?

Part 3

You will be asked some questions about more abstract issues and concepts related to the topic in Part 2. This discussion lasts between four and five minutes.

Giving gifts

On what occasions do people in your country give each other presents?

Do you feel the commercialization of gift-giving, e.g. Christmas in certain
    countries, has gone too far?

Charities

What is the role of charities nowadays?

Which charity would you like to be able to give a lot of money to?

Helping other countries

Should rich countries give much more financial assistance to poorer ones?

How can we encourage more young people to do voluntary work abroad?

Explanatory key

Test 1

Listening

Section 1

Questions 1–7 page 10

Example   touring
Keith mentions two types of bike ('touring and mountain bikes') and Jan says 'a touring bike would be best'.

1   14
Jan asks 'I'm wondering … what your prices are like'. Keith says 'the rate will be … *£14* per day'. Be careful not to confuse fou<u>rteen</u> with <u>for</u>ty.

2   1.25
When Keith mentions a 'late return fee', Jan asks him 'how much is that?' He replies 'for each additional hour it's *one pound twenty-five*'.

3   60
Keith says 'there's a deposit, too' and adds 'which you get back when you return the bicycle'. He says 'On touring models it's *£60*', which is the kind that Jan wants to rent.

4   (lightweight) bags
The cost is given but not the item, so the prompt is '£5'. Keith mentions 'accessories', and Jan asks 'Such as?' He replies 'for another £5 we can supply *lightweight bags,*' and specifies 'either panniers or the handlebar sort'.

5   lock
Jan mentions 'a pump and a repair kit' and asks if she would 'have to pay extra'. Keith answers 'no, there's no charge for things like that, or for a *lock*'. He then confirms it by mentioning a 'good strong one', referring to 'lock'.

6   100
Jan asks 'what about insurance', to which Keith responds it's 'included', but that Jan 'would have to pay part of any individual claim'. He then says 'you'd be liable for the first *£100*'. Note the further prompt 'first'.

7   credit card
Jan asks 'How do I pay?' and mentions 'cheque' and 'cash', but Keith insists on '*credit card* booking'. Both words are needed.

Questions 1–7: script

KEITH Hello … Clark's Cycle Hire. My name's Keith. How can I help you?

JAN Oh hello. I saw your ad in the local paper, and as I'm thinking of doing some cycling I'm wondering what kinds of bike you have, and what your prices are like.

KEITH Well, we hire out two main types of machine: touring and mountain bikes. Are you likely to be riding off-road, do you think?

JAN No, I'll probably be sticking to roads and country lanes, so a touring bike would be best, I think.

KEITH Right, well the rate will be £50 for a week, or **£14** per day.

JAN So it's a lot cheaper to rent by the week.

KEITH Yes definitely, though it's important to bring the bike back on time. Otherwise I'm afraid we have to charge a late return fee.

JAN And how much is that?

KEITH For each additional hour it's **one pound twenty-five**.

JAN So if you were a day late it would cost another £30?

KEITH Yes, that's right.

JAN I'd make sure I didn't do that then!

KEITH I should also point out there's a deposit, which you get back when you return the bicycle. In good condition, of course. On touring models it's **£60**.

JAN Is there anything else I'd have to pay?

KEITH No, that's it. Though if you're planning to ride fairly long distances you might like to have one or two accessories.

JAN Such as?

KEITH Well, for another £5 we can supply **lightweight bags**, either panniers or the handlebar sort. It's amazing how much they can carry, and the way they're designed means they don't get in the way when you're riding.

JAN Well, I'll see. But what about essential things like a pump, and a repair kit? I wouldn't have to pay extra for those would I?

KEITH No no, there's no charge for things like that, or for a **lock**. It's a good strong one, too. Just make sure you don't lose the key!

JAN That reminds me: what about insurance? What happens if someone steals the bike, in spite of the wonderful lock?

KEITH Didn't I mention that? I should've told you that's included in the rental, too.

JAN And it covers everything, does it?

KEITH Er … it covers you against theft of the bike, yes. As long as it's securely locked at the time. You'd have to pay part of any individual claim, though.

JAN How much?

KEITH If the bike were stolen and not recovered, you'd be liable for the first **£100**.

JAN Hmm. So, if I do go ahead and rent one, how do I pay? By cheque, or would it have to be cash?

KEITH Neither, I'm afraid. We can only accept **credit card** bookings. Otherwise we'd have to ask our customers for the full value of the machine as a deposit.

JAN I've got a Visa in my name. Would that be OK?

KEITH Sure.

Questions 8–10 page 11

8 **garage**
Keith describes the location of Oak Street as 'between the police station and a *garage* on the other side'.

9 **health centre**
He says 'go down Oak Street until you reach the health centre on the right', and that 'opposite the health centre there's a pharmacy'. The map shows the pharmacy. The answer can't be the pub: 'if you get to a pub … you've gone too far'.

10 **Clark's (Cycle Hire)**
Keith says 'we're just behind that' (i.e. the pharmacy). In this context, 'we' means 'Clark's', 'Clark's Cycle Hire' or 'Cycle Hire'. The phrase 'opposite the health centre' is a further clue.

Questions 8–10: script

JAN So if I want to have a look at the bikes, how do I find you? I live near the university, by the way.

KEITH Right. First you take Woods Road as far as the main police station …

JAN I know it. It's right next to the park

KEITH Yes, that's it. And after the police station there's a turning to the right called Oak Street …

JAN At the big supermarket?

KEITH No, it's before then. It's actually between the police station and a garage on the other side.

JAN OK.

KEITH So you go down Oak Street until you reach the health centre on the right. If you get to a pub called the Maple Leaf you've gone too far. Alright?

JAN Yes, I've got that.

KEITH Now opposite the health centre there's a pharmacy, and we're just behind that.

JAN OK, fine. I'll try to call over sometime tomorrow.

KEITH Great. See you then.

JAN Bye.

Section 2

Question 11–17 page 12

11 stamp collecting
After the prompts 'hobby and interest clubs' comes the first example, 'landscape photography', and then the answer 'stamp collecting'. Both words are needed.

12 social
After the prompt 'more than just friendship' comes the answer 'social', before the examples 'dancing' and 'speed-dating'.

13 China
You hear the prompt 'international and cultural' and then 'China' (followed by 'for instance'). Unlike in question 11, the second example comes after the answer.

14 charities
The examples, 'human rights organizations like Amnesty' and 'environmental groups such as Greenpeace' both come after the answer 'charities'.

15 political
The clues come after the answer: 'party', 'campaigning', and the first example 'Republicans'.

16 Liberal Democrats
After the example 'Republicans', the speaker mentions *Liberal Democrats* 'doing the same for their party'. Both words are needed.

17 light opera
The word 'Finally' tells you that 17 is coming. The speaker mentions 'performing arts'. The answer is the first example. The second example is 'amateur theatre'.

Questions 11–17: script

PRESENTER You're listening to Expat News, a weekly broadcast for the English-speaking community in this great city. In today's programme we'll be hearing from Tom O'Hara, who's going to tell us about all those different associations you can join. Tom.

TOM Good evening. Yes, in a city with so many of its residents born outside the country, it's hardly surprising there's such a huge range of expatriate clubs and societies. And many of these, of course, are aimed at English speakers. So first, and perhaps most obviously, we have the sports clubs, which in some cases field teams in things like rugby and tennis that compete against clubs in other parts of the country, or even abroad. You don't have to play at this level to have fun, though: they can be just a great way to do some exercise, and of course to get to know other people, especially if you're new in town. The same can be said of the many hobby and interest clubs that have sprung up here: everything from landscape photography, such as the Viewfinders club in the harbour district, or Focus on the airport road, to old favourites like **stamp collecting**. Remember that this country has a long tradition of unusual and perhaps even eccentric societies, so there should be something for everyone: a place where you can meet people of different nationalities with the same social and/or cultural interests as you. For those who may be interested in rather more than just friendship, there's a wide range of lively **social** clubs. Several singles associations organize dancing of various kinds, while for people in a real hurry there's speed-dating, in which everyone talks to everyone else for just five minutes. Then, at the end, they decide which of them they would like to meet again by ticking their names on a list. In complete contrast to these are the many religious associations, reflecting the diversity of faith groups present in this multicultural city. Many of them, of course, have their own places of worship. Perhaps also of interest to those who've come here from other parts of the world are the international and cultural societies. These often provide a meeting place for people from a specific country, **China** for instance, and particular ethnic groups, such as Afro-Caribbeans. As in other major cities, we have here local branches of many **charities** with names familiar around the world. Meetings of human rights organizations like Amnesty International are held regularly in English, as are those of environmental groups such as Greenpeace. All funds raised, by the way, go to the same kinds of good cause as they do in other countries you may have lived in. Inevitably, perhaps, there are also the **political** clubs, often connected with a particular party and, indeed, a particular country. So we have, for example, a local association of Republicans linked to and campaigning for that party in the US, and **Liberal Democrats** here doing the same for their party in Britain. Finally, on a lighter note, there's plenty to choose from in the performing arts. Whether you enjoy taking part or just watching and listening, you can take your pick from a whole range of groups. To take just a couple of examples, there's **light opera** at the Memorial Hall in the city centre, or a very lively amateur theatre company in the Park district. In summer they give open-air performances of Shakespeare plays, free of charge.

Questions 18–20 page 13

18 B

The speaker mentions 'a few associations supported by the embassies' but then states 'in the vast majority of cases it is the individual members who fund them', so B is the correct answer, not A. 'Council-subsidized sports centres' are in listeners' home countries, making C impossible.

19 B

The prompt is 'find a club'. The speaker says 'it might even determine which district of the city you decide to live in', so B is correct, not A. The speaker mentions persuading 'friends' of the need for a club, but doesn't mention choosing 'friends'. C is therefore also wrong.

20 A

The keys words are 'Then you can start your own'. Although he says 'use the local small ads on the Internet', this is 'to suggest the idea', not to join an existing club, so B is wrong. He does not suggest joining one in another town as stated in C.

Questions 18–20: script

TOM I should mention at this point that clearly some districts have a higher concentration of English-speaking clubs than others, and that certain parts of town tend to specialize in particular activities. An obvious example would be the number of water sports clubs down near the river. Whatever the number, though, they usually have one thing in common. With the exception of a few associations linked to particular countries and supported by their embassies here, in the vast majority of cases it is the individual members who fund them, so an entry fee, or a subscription, will be charged. You may be used to council-subsidized sports centres and the like in your home country, but I'm afraid that's not the case here. Assuming you can afford it, then, you can be fairly sure that somewhere out there you'll find a club that caters for your own particular fascination. If it's very important to you, and you intend to spend a lot of time on it, it might even determine which

district of the city you decide to live in. In the unlikely event that you really can't find such a club, the solution is to try to persuade friends, and anyone else you meet, of the need for one. You could also use the local small ads on the Internet to suggest the idea: you'll be amazed at just how many people share even the strangest interest. Then you can start your own.

Section 3

Questions 21–25 page 14

21 (background) reading

The tutor asks 'what you can do before you even go to the lecture'. Kareena replies 'make sure you're up to date with all the *background reading*'.

22 content

The prompt is 'check what the topic's going to be … of the lecture', but 'topic' is not the answer: the tutor's advice is to 'consider what the *content* may be'.

23 edit (notes)

The tutor asks about 'the next stage' and Kareena checks this means 'when the lecture is over'. However, 'read them' is not the answer as the tutor says 'more than that', prompting Kareena to say '*edit* them?', to which the tutor says 'Yes.'

24 next lecture

Kareena asks 'when's the best time to revise them?' and Carlos says 'just before the *next lecture*'. The tutor confirms this by saying 'Precisely' and 'that's a vital time to look at them again'.

25 week

The tutor says 'it's definitely not the only time' and asks 'when should you revise them again?'. Kareena's answer 'a month later' is not correct and the tutor recommends 'once a *week*'.

Questions 21–25: script

TUTOR Well, how are you both settling in?

CARLOS Fine.

KAREENA Yes, no problems – so far, anyway!

TUTOR Good. Remember that as your personal tutor I'm here to help you – if you do have any difficulties. Now as you know, lectures start on Monday. So I thought we'd look at a few ways of making the most of them, especially in terms of the notes you take. Let's begin by thinking about what you can do before you even go to the lecture. Any ideas?

KAREENA Make sure you're up to date with all the **background reading**, so you know plenty about the subject already?

TUTOR Yes, that's essential. The lecturer will assume you have that knowledge. Anything else, Carlos?

CARLOS Well, er, check what the topic's going to be. Of the lecture, that is.

TUTOR I'd go a bit further than that and consider what the **content** may be. Then you could ask yourself some questions that you want answering, and listen out for the relevant information during the lecture.

CARLOS OK.

TUTOR Now that brings us to the lecture itself, and the actual business of writing notes, but there's a lot to deal with there so we'll come back to that later. What I'd like to do for the moment is continue with the process of note taking, and move on to the next stage. Any suggestions for what that might be?

KAREENA When the lecture is over, you mean?

TUTOR Yes, once you're able to sit down somewhere quiet with your notes.

CARLOS Read them?

TUTOR More than that. You need to make sure they'll still make sense to you weeks, months later.

KAREENA **Edit** them?

TUTOR Yes, that's what's needed. It's well worth spending a few minutes on it. Any missing words, anything difficult to read, details you didn't have time to jot down: now is the time to do so, while everything's still fresh in your mind.

KAREENA Right. And after that, when's the best time to revise them?

TUTOR When do you think, Carlos?

CARLOS Um, I'd say just before the **next lecture**. In the same subject.

TUTOR Precisely. That's a vital time to look at them again, for obvious reasons. But it's definitely not the only time. When should you revise them again?

KAREENA A month later, maybe?

TUTOR Sooner, and much more often than that. I'd recommend you look at them again once a **week**. That's why it's so important they're complete and easy to follow.

Questions 26–29 page 15

26 at the front
The tutor asks 'What should you do when you walk into the room?' Carlos replies 'Get a good seat', before going on to say *'at the front'*. The tutor says 'Yes'.

27 leave a space
The tutor asks 'what if you don't catch something, something you know must be important?' Kareena answers *'leave a space'* and the tutor agrees with this: 'that's an excellent way to deal with it, yes'.

28 it saves time
The tutor says 'it's absolutely vital that what you write is legible', and then adds 'for one very good reason – *it saves time*'. The answer is reinforced by 'waste many hours' and 'can't read what you've written'.

29 signpost words
Here the prompts come after the answer: 'I always listen out for *signpost words*' when the tutor says 'they can tell you when something important is coming'.

Questions 26–29: script

TUTOR Right, let's go back to note-taking, and begin with the basics, before the lecture has even started. What should you do when you walk into the room?

CARLOS Get a good seat **at the front**, if you can. Where you can hear clearly and avoid distractions.

TUTOR Yes, though obviously others will have had the same idea, so it's as well to get there a bit early. So, when the lecture's under way and you're busy jotting things down, what should you try to ensure?

KAREENA That you're getting all the main points.

TUTOR And what if you don't catch something, something you know must be important?

KAREENA I'd **leave a space**, then I could check it later, perhaps by asking a question at the end, and fill it in afterwards.

TUTOR That's an excellent way to deal with it, yes. And there's something else I'd like to mention here, talking about going through notes afterwards: it's absolutely vital that what you write is legible, for one very good reason – **it saves time**. You'll waste many hours, during the course, if your revision is held up because you can't read what you've written. OK, what else can we do to make listening and note-taking more efficient?

KAREENA Well, I always listen out for **signpost words.**

CARLOS Sorry, what are they?

Kareena They're the ones lecturers use to say where they're going. A bit like a signpost at a road junction, I suppose. Things like 'the first reason is …', 'however …', 'to sum up …', and so on.

TUTOR Yes, they can tell you when something important is coming, and help you organize your notes, too.

Question 30 page 15

30 B
Carlos says 'summing up the main points in a few words' and then 'in the margin', before specifying the correct answer: 'on the left-hand side of the page'.

Question 30: script

TUTOR Is there anything else you can add, Carlos?

CARLOS Er … there's something I think is very useful, but it's later: after the lecture has finished.

TUTOR That's fine. Go on.

CARLOS Well what I do is go through what I've written down, summing up the main points in a few words in the margin, on the left-hand side of the page. I try to use words that'll jog my memory, so that I can remember what everything's about when I look at them again.

TUTOR Yes, that can work very well. What some people do to review their notes is cover up their full notes from the lecture, maybe with a piece of paper or a card, and concentrate just on what they've put in the margin, trying to recall the details. Then they move the cover down a little and check whether they were right.

KAREENA Or you could put your main points on another piece of paper and clip them together. Instead of covering and uncovering, you just hold a page in each hand.

TUTOR Sure. It's down to personal preference, really. Everyone has their own learning style.

Section 4

Questions 31–36 page 16

31 **690**
The prompt 'which lies 860 kilometres north of Adelaide' is followed by the answer '*690* south of Alice Springs'.

32 **1915**
The answer, in 'that all started to change in *1915*', comes before the prompt 'with the discovery there of opals.'

33 **First World War**
The prompt 'settlements were established' comes just before the answer 'following the *First World War*'. All three words are needed, as 'War' or 'World War' could equally apply to the 'Second World War'.

34 **Europe**
First comes the prompt 'in the late 1940s when shallow new opal fields were discovered', then 'immigrants from *Europe* arrived in large numbers'.

35 **70% / seventy per cent**
The speaker mentions 'hostile conditions' and gives examples. The recording says that 'to cope with this', 'eventually around *70%* of the town's inhabitants had made their homes beneath the surface'.

36 **shopping centre**
The prompt is 'hotels and even churches below ground', before 'an entire underground shopping centre', reinforced by 'the only one in the world'.

Questions 31–36: script

LECTURER Good afternoon. Today we're continuing this series of talks on the development of the Australian Outback with a look at Coober Pedy, the desert town of opal mines and underground living which lies 860 kilometres north of Adelaide and **690** south of Alice Springs. The inaccessibility, harsh climate and almost total lack of water made it a highly unlikely place for human habitation, but that all started to change in **1915** with the discovery there of opals, the precious stones which seem to change colour according to their surroundings. Settlements were established following the **First World War**, when soldiers returning from the trenches of France brought with them the techniques of living below ground in 'dugouts'. The Depression of the 1920s and 30s led to many prospectors leaving, but the town boomed again in the late 1940s when shallow new opal fields were discovered, and immigrants from **Europe** arrived in large numbers after the Second World War. It must be remembered, though, just how hostile conditions were. Daytime summer temperatures reached well over 50 degrees Centigrade, winter nights were bitterly cold, and dense dust storms regularly blanketed the town. To cope with this, more and more people began living in disused mines and purpose-built subterranean houses, where the temperature remains at a comfortable 25 degrees all year round, so that eventually around **70%** of the town's inhabitants had made their homes beneath the surface. This led to the construction of hotels and even churches below ground, as well as an entire underground **shopping centre**: the only one in the world.

Questions 37–40 page 17

37 **C**
The speaker says 'the nearest town to Coober Pedy is Woomera', but this doesn't mean it's near. The correct answer is C because 'even that is an enormous distance away'.

38 **A**
The speaker mentions three facilities 'within the town itself': 'hotel rooms', 'ethnic restaurants', and 'its very own opal museum'.

39 **B**
The speaker says that 'a short distance from town' we can find 'the Dingo Fence'.

40 **B**
The prompt phrase is 'another attraction'. The speaker then says that 'just outside the town' there are 'sets of various films', followed by examples.

Perhaps not surprisingly, this has now led to the emergence of a secondary industry: tourism. Increasing numbers of visitors come to see the tunnels and the caves with their ventilation shafts, the weird machines lying about in the town, and, just beyond it in the scorched red desert, the conical hills thrown up by the world's biggest opal mines. It's a logical stopping place for travellers, too. The nearest town to Coober Pedy is Woomera, in the prohibited area once used for launching space rockets, but even that is an enormous distance away. Within the town itself there are plenty of hotel rooms and a number of ethnic restaurants – remember that Coober Pedy is one of the most multicultural places in Australia, with an estimated 45 nationalities represented – and its very own opal museum. A short distance from town there's a section of the enormous barrier that runs thousands of kilometres across the country: the Dingo Fence, which is meant to keep these predatory wild dogs out of the sheep-farming areas. Another attraction just outside town are the sets of various films made there, including *Mad Max 3*, as well as *The Red Planet* and *Until the End of the World* – names that reflect the harshness of the terrain and temperatures there. The name Coober Pedy, incidentally, comes from an Aboriginal expression meaning 'white man's hole in the ground'. Next I'd like to go on to talk about Broken Hill, another mining town but one that …

Academic Reading

Passage 1

Questions 1–5 page 18

1   **Paragraph B: x**
    This paragraph explains how technological problems are no longer limiting factors. As the new constraint is 'what the human body can actually withstand', the paragraph implies that 'space biomedicine' is of increased importance.

2   **Paragraph C: ix**
    This paragraph describes 'physical changes … in zero gravity' such as thinner legs and facial swelling which are 'essentially harmless'. Therefore, this paragraph matches (ix) but not (vii), which mentions 'damage'.

3   **Paragraph D: vii**
    This paragraph lists a series of different types of harm caused when people are in space, described as 'much more serious' at the beginning. The use of 'unseen' makes (ix) impossible.

4   **Paragraph E: i**
    This paragraph begins with clues such as 'difficulties', 'accident or serious illness', 'millions of kilometres from Earth', then gives examples of these difficulties and puts forward a 'solution'.

5   **Paragraph G: vi**
    This paragraph refers to 'carrying out studies into the effects of space travel ' and then contrasts 'actually working in space' with simulating 'conditions in zero gravity', implying that the work is done 'on Earth'.

Headings not used

iii   The medical problems described in paragraph D are illnesses, not accidents. Although E does in fact mention accidents, neither this paragraph nor any other part of the text claims they are any more common in space than on Earth.

v   The references to human conditions are to those affecting the body, not the mind. There may well be psychological problems associated with these illnesses, and with simply being in space, but they are not mentioned.

viii There is in fact no mention anywhere in the text of the origins of space biomedicine, or its development up to the present day.

Questions 6 and 7 page 21

6   **(on/from) Mars**
    The second sentence in paragraph B says 'the discovery of ice *on Mars* means that there is now no necessity to design and develop a spacecraft large and powerful enough to transport the vast amounts of water needed'.

7   **they become thinner**
    The only reference in the text to 'legs' is in paragraph C. It states that the 'lower limbs become thinner'.

Questions 8–12 page 21

8   **Yes**
    The statement corresponds to the writer's comment that 'the feasibility of travel to other planets, and beyond, is no longer limited by engineering constraints but by what the human body can actually withstand'.

9   **Not given**
    There are comments on the damage done to the human body during long periods in space, but the writer does not say that astronauts will die after a specific length of time.

10 **No**
    In paragraph F, the writer states that other people have said this at some time in the past, but the writer's view contrasts with this: 'It is now clear, however, that every problem in space has a parallel problem on Earth.'

11 **Not given**
    Paragraph E mentions new techniques to 'treat internal injuries', but there is no indication that these will be any more successful in space than on Earth. The reference to 'surgeons' in paragraph F is Earth-based.

12 **No**
    In the final paragraph, the writer explains that research can, and has been, successfully carried out under water on Earth, as the need to 'simulate' the conditions in space makes clear. For the same reason, the 'bed' would also be on earth.

Questions 13 and 14 page 22

13 communicate with patients
The information is in paragraph F. The writer mentions telemedicine 'for treating astronauts in space' and goes on to state that it can be used to '*communicate with patients* in remote parts of the world.'

14 filter contaminated water
The information is in paragraph F. The writer mentions 'sterilizing waste water' in space and goes on to state that this can be used to '*filter contaminated water* at the scene of natural disasters.'

Passage 2

Questions 15–19 page 25

15 (deep) canyons
The third paragraph (lines 18–32) uses the expressions 'the 1960s', 'discovered' and 'in the rock at the bottom of the sea' (bedrock), so 'canyons' or 'deep canyons' is the correct answer.

16 above
The third paragraph (lines 18–32) says 'river erosion of bedrock cannot occur below sea level', but rivers flowing into the Mediterranean had cut into this rock. It states that the same is true of caves. Therefore, when the summary refers back to these features, it is saying that both canyons and caves must have been formed *above* sea level.

17 sea floor
The fourth paragraph mentions a subsequent examination in 1970 (lines 35–36) 'to study the *sea floor* near the Spanish island of Majorca', so the missing expression is '*sea floor*', with more proof in the next sentence.

18 shellfish
The fourth paragraph mentions 'samples' which were 'two kilometres below' (line 39). The samples contained two kinds of living things: vegetation ('plants') and '*shellfish*'. This is reinforced by the adjective 'shallow-water'.

19 silt/sand and mud
The phrase 'as well as' in the summary tells you that 19 was also inside the samples, and the reference to 'once … carried by river water' (lines

43–44) parallels the phrase 'originally transported by river' in the summary, so the answer must be 'silt', or 'sand and mud'.

Questions 20–22 page 26

20 E
The relevant part of the text is 'The ice reflects sunlight into space' (line 67–68). The consequence of this is that 'the planet cools'.

21 F
The clue is in line 73 – 'the water flowed faster and faster.' The previous sentence says it is 'ocean water'. Before that, the text says 'the gap enlarged' and makes comparisons with 'Victoria Falls' and 'Niagara', making it clear that F is the right answer.

22 B
The clue is 'reheating the oceans and the planet' (lines 82–83). Just before that, the text says that 'waters of the vast inland sea drowned the falls and warm water began to escape to the Atlantic.' F is not possible because the water flowing over the falls was going the opposite way.

Questions 23–27 page 27

23 D
The text says 'the deep outward flow from sea to ocean was progressively cut off' (lines 52–54), so D is correct. A is false because the text says 'gradually cut off', not 'suddenly closed'. For B, there is no mention in the text of any fall in the level of the Atlantic. C is false because the 'shallow inward flow of ocean water into the Mediterranean' remained until 'the shallow opening at Gibraltar finally closed completely', so *immediately* is wrong.

24 A
The key part is 'the sea became more *saline* and creatures that couldn't handle the rising *salt* content perished … except for bacteria' (lines 56–59). B uses a word from the text – 'bacteria' – but wrongly makes it the cause. C may be true, but there is no indication that this killed plants or animals in the Mediterranean. D is also true, but this occurred after most life in the sea had already died, so it was not a cause.

25 B

The salinity crisis was said early in the text to have 'plunged the Earth into an ice age', so when it ended 5.4 million years ago, the 'reheating' referred to in line 82 meant the end of an ice age too. A is contradicted by 'reheating of the planet'. C indicates 'Victoria Falls/Niagara' but misinterprets the text. D is not supported anywhere in the text.

26 C

The prompt is 'Subsequent', with the evidence 'some believe … that the Mediterranean must have dried up and refilled many times' (lines 88–90). A exaggerates what the text says: 'added a few wrinkles to Ryan and Hsu's scenario'. For B, the studies did not disprove their main argument, only the 'details'. D is not suggested in the text.

27 D

The phrase 'not something our species has to worry about' (line 98) implies that humans will no longer exist when 'nature's closure' occurs. A is incorrect because the phrase 'If continental drift does reseal the Mediterranean' means it is possible. B is incorrect because, although there is a lighthearted mention of 'stockpiling dynamite', there is no serious suggestion of technological measures to stop it happening. C is similar to A: 'if' means it is possible but not certain.

Reading passage 3

Questions 28–31   page 30

28 F

Paragraph F describes the process of becoming different in appearance: 'admission of certain wolves … and exclusion of larger, more threatening ones led to the development of people-friendly breeds distinguishable from wolves by size, shape, coat, ears, and markings.'

29 J

The final paragraph mentions 'prized bloodlines' and organizations: one 'registers 150 breeds', one 'lists 196' and another 'recognizes many more'.

30 A

Paragraph A makes the point several times: 'dogs remain as similar [to wolves] as humans … are to each other … not much different at all'; 'dogs and wolves differ by not much more than one per cent'.

31 I

This paragraph refers to a king 'said to love his dogs more than his subjects 'and to a relative of another king who shouted 'save the dogs' when 'sailors drowned'.

Questions 32–35   pages 30–31

B, C, F, H (any order)

B   Paragraph B mentions '*before* the development of … *permanent* human settlements', while paragraph D mention '*wandering* packs … and … *nomadic* humans'.

C   Paragraph C refers to 'the most *suppliant* wolves', while paragraph F mentions 'wolves that would know the tricks of *subservience and could adapt to humans in charge*.'

F   Paragraph F talks of 'animals … *scavenging leftovers*' (i.e. eating anything the humans didn't want).

H   Paragraph F states that 'Puppies in particular would be *hard to resist*.'

Not used

A   Paragraph C describes 'the similar … size of wolf packs and early human clans', while paragraph D mentions 'packs of 25 or 30 wolves and clans of like-numbered … humans'.

D Paragraph D states 'certain wolves' were accepted 'into early human gatherings ... by proving ... unthreatening'.

E Paragraph F states 'food would have been plentiful.'

G Paragraph B states that archaeological evidence 'puts wolves ... in the company of man ... before the development of farming'

Questions 36–40 page 31

36 D
The second sentence of paragraph H talks about 'Roman warriors' who 'trained large dogs for battle'. The next sentence describes how 'the brutes' could attack 'an armed man'.

37 E
Paragraph I refers to dogs in 'seventeenth century England' used as a source of energy: 'pulling carts ...', 'working as turn-spits' and 'powering wheels ...'.

38 F
The last sentence in paragraph G says 'Native Americans among others ate puppies'. Neither the 'others' alluded to here, nor the 'societies' in the next clause, are mentioned by name.

39 A
Although hunting is referred to in B, C, D and G, paragraph H refers specifically to ancient Greece, where people used 'speedy Laconians ... to chase and kill rabbits and deer.'

40 E
This is the second use of E. Paragraph I refers to 'herding livestock' in England, e.g. working as sheepdogs.

Test 2

Listening

Section 1

Questions 1–6 page 42

1 A Yes, definitely
The prompt is 'the next thing is the gas supply'. Simon asks 'Do you have a safety certificate?' and then specifies 'a current one'. The owner replies 'We do'.

2 A Yes, definitely
Simon asks 'When did they actually do the inspection?', to which the owner eventually replies 'just over five months ago'. Her first answer is 'early last year', but she then corrects this.

3 B Maybe
Simon asks 'And the electricity. When was the last time all the wiring was inspected?' Although the owner remembers an 'electrician' in flat 3A, she can't remember 'if he looked at everything then.' She offers to 'find the bill and check.'

4 C Definitely not
Simon asks 'are there enough plug sockets in the flat?' and they then discuss the meaning of 'enough' in this context. The owner says one per room and Simon's lighthearted 'I'll take that as a "no" then,' is confirmed by the owner's answer 'All right'.

5 B Maybe
Simon asks about a 'smoke alarm'. Although the owner says 'yes', that only partly answers question 5. Simon's follow-up question 'is it in good working order?' brings the response 'I'll have to try it out, and let you know,' so there is no certainty.

6 A Yes, definitely
Simon talks about 'the previous tenants' and then asks if any tenants 'still have keys to the door'. The owner is definite about this: 'everyone has to hand back the keys … and those in 3A have always done so.'

Questions 1–6: script

SIMON Hello, this is Simon Marshall. I spoke to you the other day about renting flat 3A.

OWNER Oh yes, hello Simon. What can I do for you?

SIMON Well, there are a few health and safety things I'd like to run through if that's OK.

OWNER Yes, fine.

SIMON Right, well the first thing, bearing in mind it's quite an old house, is whether there's any damp. I'm thinking here of the exterior walls, and the floor.

OWNER Well, I've never known any problems with damp there. It was all right last time I checked, certainly – though that was before the recent wet weather. I'd better have another look and get back to you on that.

SIMON OK. Now the next thing is the gas supply. Do you have a safety certificate? A current one that is.

OWNER We do. All the gas appliances have been checked by a registered engineer.

SIMON Yes, I was going to ask about that. When did they actually do the inspection?

OWNER Let me think … they sent an engineer to check something early last year, but, no, that wasn't the inspection … Oh I remember now, it was in the Spring. In fact I've got the certificate here somewhere … yes, that's it: March 22nd, so it's just over five months ago.

SIMON And the electricity. When was the last time all the wiring was inspected? I know it doesn't have to be checked as often as the gas, but it's still important, especially in older properties.

OWNER As it happens we had an electrician in when we redecorated flat 3A. If he looked at everything then, he would have charged us for it. I'll find the bill and check it if you like.

SIMON Fine. And when was that?

OWNER Er … the decorators finished just before Easter, so that would be about eighteen months ago.

SIMON Just one more point on the electrics: are there enough plug sockets in the flat?

OWNER It depends what you mean by 'enough' really.

SIMON Well I've got quite a lot of electrical things – computer, radio, lamps, kitchen appliances and so on – and I'm wondering whether I could plug them all in without having cables trailing all over the place.

OWNER I think there's one per room: that's fairly normal in older properties.

SIMON I'll take that as a 'no' then!

OWNER All right.

SIMON Now, another safety point: is there a smoke alarm?

OWNER Yes, there's one in the kitchen.

SIMON And is it in good working order?

OWNER I'll have to try it out, and let you know.

SIMON Right. Now you mentioned the previous tenants: do they, or anyone else who's lived in the flat, still have keys to the door?

OWNER We're very strict about that. Everyone has to hand back the keys when they leave, or we don't return the deposit. And those in 3A have always done so.

Questions 7–10 page 43

7 C
Simon talks about 'a room where people can leave things' and asks 'Where exactly is that? Is it next to 3A … on the third floor?' The owner replies that 'the apartment's on the third, yes, but the storeroom's a little way away,' to which Simon asks 'it's on the same floor, isn't it?' The owner replies 'Yes, it is.'

8 B
The word '70s' refers to when the heating was installed, not the temperature. Although 55 *is* a temperature, it's not the present one: 'it used to be set at 55.' The correct answer is 'it's a constant 60 degrees.'

9 C
Don't confuse the size of the yard ('20 square metres') with that of the garden: 'about 150 metres'. Other figures to be careful with are the size of the motorbike engine ('50 cc') and the old man's age ('nearly 90').

10 B
The owner first says '70 cm' but then corrects herself by saying 'No, sorry, that was the old one. This one's 80.' 90 is the number of channels available.

Questions 7–10: script

SIMON OK. Now there are a few other practical details. Firstly, you mentioned a room where people can leave things like suitcases and bags and things. Where exactly is that? Is it next to 3A, which I take it is on the third floor?

OWNER Well the apartment's on the third, yes, but the storeroom's a little way away, just past the second door to the right. Under the stairs, in fact.

SIMON But it's on the same floor, isn't it?

OWNER Yes, it is.

SIMON Fine. Now another thing I wanted to check is that there's hot water in the apartment.

OWNER Oh yes, it runs off the central heating – that was installed back in the 70s I think – so there's a permanent supply.

SIMON But is it really hot? Not just warm, or lukewarm.

OWNER I suppose it depends what you mean by hot, but it's at a constant 60 degrees.

SIMON That sounds fine.

OWNER Yes, it used to be set at 55, but last year the tenants asked us to increase it, so we did.

SIMON I'm glad about that! OK, now can you tell me a bit about the yard, and the garden? How big are they?

OWNER Well the yard, at the side of the house, is about 20 square metres.

SIMON Oh, so there's room for my motorbike, then. Actually it's only a 50 cc moped, but I like to keep it off the road at night.

OWNER Yes, there's more than enough space there, even with all the wheelie bins.

SIMON And the garden?

OWNER That's much bigger. About 150 square metres.

SIMON Who looks after it, by the way?

OWNER Old Mr Collins. He's almost 90 but he's out there every day.

SIMON And the last point: the TV. What size screen is it?

OWNER It's 70 centimetres wide, I think. No, sorry, that was the old one. This one's 80. You can get ninety-odd channels on it, so I'm told.

SIMON Really? So there's a satellite dish on the roof, is there?

OWNER No. it's cable TV here. It doesn't cost much between everyone, though.

SIMON That's very interesting. OK, thanks for your help. I'll be in touch again soon.

OWNER Thank you. Bye for now.

SIMON Bye.

Section 2

Questions 11 and 12 page 44

11 B

The prompt is the reference to a 'survey'. The figure of 32% is given for the number of students 'coping with loneliness'. Be careful not to mishear sixteen hundred as a percentage and choose A. Don't interpret 32% to mean people who do not suffer loneliness, which would give answer C.

12 A

Although you hear the prompt 'report by researchers' and then 'personal welfare and health services', you have to wait until the speaker says '61% of all people using counselling services were aged under 30.' B is wrong because '30' is not a percentage. The figure 57% is only for 'men' included within the 61% already mentioned.

Questions 11 and 12: script

COUNSELLOR Loneliness is something we all suffer from in varying degrees, but young people living on their own can be particularly vulnerable. Many who leave the family home find they are less confident and have more difficulty in finding their feet than they expected. Often, going to work or study in another town or city will be the first time they have lived away from home. Although this may sound like an adventure for those dying to get away from the glare of the parental eye, for others it is a daunting prospect which generates apprehension, uncertainty, and even fear. In fact, in a recent survey of over sixteen hundred people who had recently left home, 32% said that understanding and coping with loneliness was a crucial issue for them and made them feel highly stressed and distracted. An annual report by researchers last year recorded a noticeable increase in the number of individuals with homesickness, transition, and isolation issues. Acknowledging that feelings of loneliness and isolation could impede progress at work or study, they examined the number of people using the welfare and health services. They found that young people in particular were prone to difficulties. Last year 61% of all people using counselling services were aged under 30 and of this group, 57% were men.

Questions 13–20 page 45

13 first year

The first prompt is 'Leaving home'. The speaker describes causes of loneliness, then says 'For this reason, in the *first year* a lot of young people suffer from loneliness.'

14 (other) people

The word 'Ironically' is a clue. The speaker contrasts a 'sense of isolation' with being 'surrounded by *people* most of the time', and 'constantly among *people*' with 'a sense of being alone'.

15 on their own

The speaker say 'It is often those who are more used to being *on their own* who deal best with the transitional period of leaving home.'

16 primary school

The sentence 'It may be the first time you have had to make new friends since you started *primary school*' expresses the same idea as the statement.

17 far (away)

The prompt here is 'long-distance relationship'. The text refers to 'that special person who lives so *far away*.'

18 everyone/everybody

The prompt here is the sentence 'One of the ways of combating loneliness is to remember that it's not your fault'. The speaker says '*everyone* has to deal with (it)'.

19 activities

The question paraphrases the part of the text that says people can 'get involved in *activities* which interest them as a way of meeting more people.'

20 support services

The prompts are the word 'counselling' and 'For more information'. The speaker says 'contact the town hall's *support services*.'

Questions 13–20

COUNSELLOR: Leaving home involves a major change in lifestyle, work patterns and degree of independence. You will be away from home, family and friends and are no longer supported by familiar surroundings. For this reason, in the **first year** a lot of young people suffer from loneliness. Ironically, this sense of isolation comes at a time when you are likely to be surrounded by **people** most of the time. Living in a busy city, travelling on crowded buses and trains, you will be constantly among people, but this can sometimes compound your sense of being alone. Seeing others who appear at ease among large crowds, mingling and making friends, can make you feel excluded and inadequate. Adapting to a new environment makes people uncertain of what to do or how to behave and breeds insecurities which can make for a real sense of isolation. It is often those who are more used to being **on their own** who deal best with the transitional period of leaving home. Other reasons for feeling alone include high expectations of the big city where you have 'the best time of your life' and meet 'lifelong friends'. It may be the first time you have had to make new friends since you started **primary school** and perhaps you are reluctant or finding it hard to replace old friends whom you miss. There are also pressures to juggle work and socializing which may leave you feeling left out, or it could be that you have a long distance relationship and feel torn between your new lifestyle and that special person who lives so **far away**. Because loneliness can leave you with a sense of low self-esteem where you become self-conscious and feel you have been rejected, it is very difficult to overcome. You may be reluctant to even try and make new friends or take part in social activities, and will also find it difficult to say 'no' to things, leaving you feeling exploited and weak. One of the ways of combating loneliness is to remember that it's not your fault, and that it's something **everyone** has to deal with, despite appearances. Counsellors advise those feeling lonely to speak to someone they know about their feelings. They also ask them to consider joining groups and societies and to get involved in **activities** which interest them as a way of meeting more people. Of course, overdoing it and jamming your schedule with too many things just to avoid being alone will not work, but meeting others with common interests may be a step forward. If you still feel like you need someone to talk to, you could try group counselling where you will be able to talk to and receive support from a small number of people with the same difficulties as you. For more information, or to be put in touch with an individual counsellor, contact the local town hall's **support services**.

Section 3

Questions 21–24 page 46

21–23 A, E, F (any order)

A Paul asks A directly, 'Is it near the College?', and Katy's answer means 'yes': 'just round the corner from here'.

E When talking about PCs, Katy refers to 'materials in over fifteen different languages'.

F Katy says 'the same hardware (i.e. Macintosh and PC) permits access to the Internet with its many language learning and discussion sites.'

Incorrect options

B Katy says the 'books … audio or video cassettes' are 'at a wide range of levels of difficulty.'

C Katy refers to 'reference books without tapes'.

D Katy talks about 'daily' newspapers, but the Centre in fact receives the 'weekly international edition of the Spanish newspaper *El Pais*.'

24 C, D (any order)

The first prompt is Paula's question 'What about TV?', followed by Katy's mention of 'the second floor'. Katy talks of 'televisions to view live satellite television broadcasts in seven languages' and then lists these.

C Katy mentions Turkish after the main list – 'Turkish broadcasting can be viewed live on request'.

D Katy says that 'The Centre records the news in French, German, Arabic …'

Incorrect options

A English is not included in the first list.

B Japanese is not included in the first list.

E Portuguese is mentioned in the first list of live broadcasts, but not among the list of news recordings.

Questions 21–24: script

KATY Hi, I'm Katy Shaw and I work at the University Language Centre. Your tutor tells me you might be interested in using the Centre, so I'm here at the College to explain a bit about it and of course to answer your questions.

PAULA Where exactly is the Centre? Is it near the College?

KATY It's actually on King's Road: just round the corner from here, in fact.

JEFF Oh I know it, yes. I wondered what that building was.

STEVE Yes, what's there?

KATY Well, the library has about 4000 books, pamphlets and transcripts to go with some of the 12,500 items on audio or video cassettes. These are at a wide range of levels of difficulty, covering language learning material in over 100 languages. There are also reference books without tapes including dictionaries, grammars, grammar workbooks, vocabulary workbooks and model letters, as well as texts on academic writing and effective study habits, etc. Audio cassette workrooms are on the first floor, by the way.

STEVE Do they get any foreign-language press there, too?

KATY Yes, the library subscribes to a number of European daily and weekly newspapers including *Le Monde* from France, *L'Espresso* from Italy and the weekly international edition of the Spanish paper *El Pais*.

JEFF What about learning with computers? Can you do that there?

KATY CALL, or Computer Aided Language Learning, is available on the first floor.

JEFF How many PC's are there?

KATY Counting both Macintosh and PC platforms, there are nine at present. There are materials in over fifteen different languages, and new material and language categories are being added as library funds permit. The programs cover verb drills, grammar exercises, activities to accompany multi-media textbooks, pronunciation, translation and some multi-media applications. The same hardware permits access to the Internet with its many language learning and discussion sites.

PAULA What about TV? That's a good way of learning a language too.

KATY Yes, definitely. We agree. So on the second floor of the Centre there are televisions to view live satellite television broadcasts in seven languages.

PAULA Which ones are they?

KATY Currently, we've got Arabic, French, German,

Italian, Portuguese, Spanish and Russian. Turkish broadcasting can be viewed live on request. The Centre records the news in French, German, Arabic, Italian, Japanese, Spanish and Russian. And English, too.

Question 25–30 page 47

25–27 B, E, F (any order)

B The prompt is from Paula: 'How do we sign up?' Katy says 'you need to go to the Centre with a valid University ID or a letter … indicating your status'.

E Steve asks 'Are there any forms to fill in?', to which Katy replies 'I'm afraid so', and then specifies 'at the ground floor Reception Desk'. She then confirms E by referring to 'registration'.

F Katy refers to the 'need to take part in an induction' into 'proper operation of the Centre's computers, televisions, videos'.

Incorrect options

A Katy says you can '*avoid* paying a fee.'

C Although she mentions a 'Departmental Administrator', this is in the context of writing the letter.

D There is a reference to 'language requirements', but this means the student's requirements, not the Centre's. There is, therefore, no need to 'take a test'.

28 A, B

Although Katy says 'tell the librarian who you are on your first visit', this is not one of the options in 28.

A The first relevant reference is when Katy says 'let her (the librarian) know what – if any – knowledge of it (the language) you already have.'

B Katy tells the others to 'say what reasons you have for learning the language.'

Incorrect options

C Katy explains that the librarian will 'offer you advice on how much time is needed to make progress in the language.'

D Katy explains that the librarian will 'help you make the best choice of books.'

E Katy refers to 'suggestions on how to improve your language learning techniques', but does not mention 'other languages you have learned.'

29–30 Answers A, E (any order)

A The prompts are Jeff's questions 'Can she copy tapes for us to take home? Or can we borrow them?' Katy says 'the library is a resource centre and reference library only', but makes it clear that A is correct when she says 'you can do as much self-study listening and reading work there as you want.'

E Katy's comment 'international copyright law prohibits users from copying more than 5% of any one title in the academic year' implies that some pages may be copied.

Incorrect options

B Katy rules out taking books away: 'it's not possible to take home materials, that's to say books or cassettes.'

C Katy rules out copying tapes: 'copyright law doesn't permit the library or its staff to make copies of cassettes for use by students outside the Centre.'

D Steve asks 'is it OK to photocopy them?' to which Katy replies 'the library staff will handle any photocopying.' This makes D impossible, confirmed by 'you place a photocopy order with the librarian.'

Questions 25–30: script

PAULA Sounds great. How do we sign up?

KATY To avoid paying a fee, you need to go to the Centre with a valid University ID card, or a letter from your College or Departmental Administrator on headed paper indicating your status, length of stay and language requirements.

STEVE Are there any forms to fill in?

KATY I'm afraid so! You do that at the ground floor Reception Desk. Your registration is for one academic year only and needs to be renewed annually. You should tell the librarian who you are on your first visit, and you will need to take part in an induction to the library service, including the proper operation of the Centre's computers, televisions, videos and so on.

PAULA Can she help us choose the right materials, too?

KATY Yes! The librarian can give advice and assistance in locating material, making best use of the texts and tapes, and so on. Let her know which language you want to study and what – if any – knowledge of it you already have. Also say what reasons you have for learning the language. Your answers will help the librarian help you make the best choice of books and tapes for your needs. She can also offer you advice on how much time is needed to make progress in the language, and can offer suggestions on how to improve your language learning techniques.

JEFF Can she copy tapes for us to take home? Or can we borrow them?

KATY The library is a resource centre and reference library only. You can do as much self-study listening and reading work there as you want, but it's not possible to take home materials, that's to say books or cassettes. And copyright law doesn't permit the library or its staff to make copies of cassettes for use by students outside the Centre. All material must be used on the premises, I'm afraid. This ensures that materials are always available for students working on their own and not out on loan for long periods, which could harm users' progress.

STEVE So if we can't take books home, is it OK to photocopy them?

KATY The library staff will handle any photocopying, though international copyright law prohibits users from copying more than 5% of any one title in the academic year. You place a photocopy order with the librarian or an assistant and orders will be processed between one and two o'clock, or after five thirty.

PAULA How much does it cost?

KATY Ten pence per page. Payment is by photocopy card, which you can buy from the Information Desk on the ground floor….

Section 4

Questions 31–34 page 48

31 (the) US/USA/America
The year '1893' is mentioned and 'Whitcomb Judson' is referred to as 'another American inventor who took … the Clasp Locker … to the World's Fair … in *the US*.'

32 success
The first clue comes before the 'Hookless Fastener' is mentioned: 'the buying public began to take an interest'. Following the reference to 'Sundback', the speaker confirms the answer: 'it sold quite well'.

33 1919
Both 'Kynoch' and the 'Ready Fastener' are heard before the date 'in *1919*'.

34 Goodrich's
The speaker says that 'the Zipper' was 'designed and given its modern American name by BF *Goodrich*.' The surname is repeated and there is a play on words: 'made Mr *Goodrich* extremely rich indeed'.

Questions 31–34

LECTURER I think you all have a copy of the printed notes and diagram … but I should point out before we go any further that there are a few mistakes in those notes, so please correct any you notice as we go along. Right, as you can see, we are going to be looking at the zip, or zipper as it's known in the **US**, which is where it had its origins in 1851. In fact, it was initially given the rather less catchy name of the Automatic Continuous Clothing Closure by the person that invented it: Elias Howe, who also designed the first sewing machine. It wasn't until 1893, though, that someone actually tried to market the zip, when Whitcomb Judson, another American inventor, took what he called the Clasp Locker to the World's Fair held that year in the US. His hook and eye system was a commercial disaster, and it was another fifteen years before the buying public began to take an interest: this time a more reliable model with facing sets of teeth named the Hookless Fastener, designed by a Swedish engineer called Gideon Sundback. Attached to clothing, purses and other items, **it sold quite well**. Gradually this new alternative to buttons caught on, as people realized the advantages of a fastener that only needed one hand to operate, that children could use, that left no visible gaps, and so on. The British firm Kynoch began producing and selling the Ready Fastener in large numbers in **1919**, and a few years later the Zipper, designed and given its modern American name by BF **Goodrich**, made Mr **Goodrich** extremely rich indeed.

Questions 35–39 page 49

35 pin
The prompt for the diagram is 'Let's look first at the right-hand side of the illustration'. The description goes clockwise from 'tape' to 'heat seal patch' to 'alongside the heat seal patch is a small piece of metal … to enable the two halves of the zip to join.' The speaker states 'this is known as the *pin*'.

36 box
Details on 36 are given: 'opposite that, on the other half of the zip in the diagram, is a device which correctly aligns the pin.' This is then identified: 'the *box*, as it's called, begins the joining of the zip halves.'

37 (metal) teeth
The answer must be plural: 'running up the inside edge of each half are dozens, possibly hundreds, of *metal teeth*.' There is a second reference: 'moving up and down the *teeth* …'

38 pull tab
The prompt is the reference to 'a piece of metal called the slider'. The speaker says 'this is operated by means of a *pull tab*,' and then confirms the first word: 'the wearer or user pulls it.'

39 top stop
The speaker gives the prompt 'to prevent the slider coming off the teeth at the other end,' before specifying that 'there is a *top stop* on both sides of the zip.' Study of the diagram will confirm this last point.

Question 40 page 49

40 B
In B, 'outline' indicates only the most important points, while 'development' covers both the brief historical background and the description of the 'still widely used' separable zip. A overstates the scope of the talk: only one kind of zip fastener is explained. Although the second part of the text focuses on one kind of zip, as stated in C, the speaker has no commercial motive: the only particular makes he mentions were last made in the 1920s. The speaker briefly refers to the zip's 'occasional tendency to trap parts of the wearer's anatomy', but this is the only, passing, mention of the 'dangers' in D.

Questions 35–40: script

LECTURER If its use in trousers was a major factor in establishing the zip as a fashion icon, despite its occasional tendency to trap parts of the wearer's anatomy, another major breakthrough came with the separable zip: the kind that opens at both ends. This type, still widely used in a range of items from jackets to tents, is shown in the diagram. Let's look first at the right-hand side of the illustration, at the material attached to the item of clothing, the bag or whatever. This is the tape, which is usually made of fairly tough fabric. At the end of that there's what is known as the heat seal patch: the cotton and nylon laminated material used to reinforce the tape. Now alongside the heat seal patch is a small piece of metal, used only on a separating zip, whose function is to enable the two halves of the zip to join. This is known as the '**pin**'. Opposite that, on the other half of the zip in the diagram, is a device which correctly aligns the pin. The '**box**', as it's called, begins the joining of the zip halves. Running up the inside edge of each half are dozens, possibly hundreds, of metal '**teeth**', each of which has a small hook and an equally tiny hollow. Moving up and down the teeth, to open and close the zip, is a piece of metal called the slider. This is operated by means of a '**pull tab**', so called because, logically enough, the wearer or user pulls it in one direction or the other. To close the zip, a wedge inside the slider pushes the hook of each tooth on one side into the hollow of each offset tooth on the other; to open it, the wedge forces them apart. To prevent the slider coming off the teeth at the other end, there is a '**top stop**' on both sides of the zip. This basic design has changed little in the many years since it was first introduced, although nowadays, of course, zips – zippers – are available in a whole range of shapes, sizes and materials.

Academic reading

Passage 1

Questions 1–5 page 51

1 **B**
The textile factory is mainly mentioned from line 25 where 'workers complained of being bitten.' It states that 'dermatitis swept through the workplace' and 'seemed to be transmitted through employees' social groups.'

2 **C**
Line 34 mentions an 'infestation' that 'spread through office staff going through dusty records that had lain untouched for decades.' In line 76 there is further evidence: 'clerical staff poring over records.'

3 **A**
Lines 11–13 refer to the laboratory where there was 'a problem, attributed to cable mites', and says that 'a concerted effort was made to exterminate the mites.'

4 **B**
This refers to the factory again. Lines 26–28 state that 'workers complained of being bitten by insects brought into the factory in imported cloth.'

5 **A**
This refers to the laboratory again. Lines 11–13 state 'that the problem … started to spread to relatives of the victims.'

Questions 6–8 page 52

6 **individual scratching**
Lines 53–67 relate to the chart. The chart requires the cause of group scratching. The text says that 'individual scratching' would 'prime them (the group) to scratch itches of their own' (cause/effect).

7 **alerted others**
This is given as a consequence of 'individual scratching'. It would have 'alerted others that there were biting insects or parasites present.' The phrase 'biting insects or parasites' corresponds to 'pests' in the chart.

8 **bonding**
In the text, the 'necessary bonding' is given as a beneficial consequence of 'mutual grooming.'

Questions 9–13 page 53

9 **F**
The reference is in lines 71–73: 'people may unconsciously exaggerate symptoms … because it gets them a break from unappealing work.' However, the text says 'unconsciously', while the question reads 'they know it will.'

10 **T**
The text says that 'the lab workers … spent the day laboriously examining the results of … tests' and 'textile workers and clerical staff … found what they had to do tedious' (lines 73–78). Both 'laboriously' and 'tedious' indicate 'boring'.

11 **NG**
You might reasonably assume this to be true, but it isn't mentioned anywhere in the text, despite the overall topic.

12 **T**
The text states 'few will accept … what psychologists call a hysterical condition. In the past … expert reassurance was enough; these days there is a mistrust of conventional medicine' (lines 84–89).

13 **F**
The prompt is Internet in line 92, followed by the mention of 'an epidemic'. However, the final sentence says 'Only an awareness of the power of the illusion can stop it.'

Question 14 page 53

14 **D**
The gist is that certain parasites and insect bites are all in the mind. Option A only relates to the content of paragraph 7; B only to paragraphs 2, 4, and 5; C mentions 'scratching', part of the main theme, but 'yawning' and 'laughing' are only incidental references in the text; E relates only to the final part of the text.

Passage 2

Questions 15–19 page 54

15 Section II: i
The reference 'completed in 1875' makes it clear this was the original lift. The second and third paragraphs of this section, beginning 'the operating mechanism consisted of …', explain how it worked.

16 Section III: e
The first paragraph of this section states the problems of 'pitting and grooving of the cylinders and pistons' and their cause, while the second describes the attempted remedies and effect. It also mentions a problem with 'the boiler for the steam engine'.

17 Section IV: h
The first paragraph of this section describes the structure added to the original, which included 'the A-frames', 'the platform' and 'the new operating mechanism'. The way this machinery worked is discussed in the second paragraph.

18 Section V: a
The only section which says what the lift was actually used for is V. The first paragraph of this section considers its use with cargo vessels, and the second, its tourism function.

19 Section VI: c
Clues include the contrast with 'demolition' and words such as 'save' and 'conserved'. Although the second paragraph of this section mentions 'replacing' and a 'replica', the third explains that they in fact restored the lift to its 1875 system and structure.

Not used
b covers too many sections – II, III & IV.

d deals only with the first thing mentioned in the text.

g is too narrow: only the first paragraph of section IV discusses the supports.

j is incorrect because at no stage is there a 'completely new lift': the second is built on top of the first, and the third returns to the structure and operating system of the first.

Questions 20–24 page 57

20 platform
The answer to 17 indicates that the relevant section is IV. The first paragraph of section IV describes 'the *platform* that now formed the top of the framework: on it was located the new operating mechanism, which included seventy-two pulleys.'

21 A-frame
As 'the platform … formed the top of the framework', you can see what was there 'to support' this platform: the A-shaped structures 'at either side'.

22 pulley(s)
The pulleys are mentioned as part of the 'operating mechanism' on the 'platform', and again when describing how the 'wire ropes … ran … around pulleys.'

23 (boat carrying) tank
The tanks are the biggest moving parts in the diagram, able to be 'raised or lowered'. The explanation of the mechanism – the ropes running around the 'pulleys' – provides further clues.

24 (cast iron) weights
Their location is given – 'at the side of the structure' – and their connection to the tanks via the pulleys is described in the first sentence of the second paragraph.

Questions 25–27 page 58

25 France and Belgium
In Section II, the text states that 'the lift became a prototype for larger versions … in *France and Belgium*.'

26 a hydraulic pump
In Section II, the text states that '*a hydraulic pump* driven by steam supplied … additional energy … to effect … movement.'

27 cylinders and pistons
The first paragraph of Section III states that 'the canal water used' was 'corrosive, and therefore causing the damage.' The 'damage' refers back to 'the pitting and grooving of the *cylinders and pistons*'.

Passage 3

Questions 28–34 page 61

28 size

The summary covers lines 58–79. Question 28 requires a noun meaning 'the tiniest … to the biggest'. The one from the list that fits is *size*.

29 never

An adverb is required. The text says 'this kind of life is all we know' (lines 63–64), which paraphrases the summary 'we have *never* observed any other kinds of organism'.

30 mistake

A noun is needed, probably in a fixed expression. The text says 'scientists … tend to look for … vital signs that betray earthly organisms when we have absolutely no reason for thinking that life elsewhere should be earthlike' (lines 66–70). In other words, they are making a *mistake* (not a 'breakthrough').

31 planet

Following 'another', this must be a singular noun. The text refers to 'Mars' and 'Martian meteorites', which refer to a planet, not an entire galaxy.

32 narrow

An adjective is required to qualify 'definition'. This word appears twice in the text: on the first occasion the writer is concerned that the definition 'cannot be based more broadly' (line 71), i.e. that it is *narrow*. There is no suggestion that the scientists' definition has changed since the previous one.

33 composition

This needs a plural or uncountable noun contrasting with 'behaviour'. This part of the summary relates to the phrase in the text 'what it does, rather than what it is made of' (lines 75–76): the word that means 'what it is made of' is *composition*.

34 defining

A verb -ing form is required. The answer relates to lines 76-79: 'it is difficult … to make such a definition stick, preventing the term from becoming so inclusive as to be meaningless.'

Questions 35–38 page 62

35 C

The question paraphrases the sentence 'But as Cohen and Stewart show in their novel, it is possible to imagine entities … which appear to be alive, but which bear absolutely no resemblance to terrestrial organisms' (lines 90–94).

36 A

The question paraphrases the sentence 'Aliens, he (Aldiss) argues, are a manifestation of a fundamental human urge to populate the universe with "others"' (lines 43–45).

37 B

The question paraphrases the sentence 'In his latest novel … Banks describes organisms the size of continents supporting entire civilizations as their intestinal parasites' (lines 111–114).

38 C

The question has a similar meaning to the sentence 'Their argument with astrobiology is not that aliens might not exist, but that we (humans) cannot help be constrained in our search' (lines 55–57).

Questions 39–40 page 63

39 A

The writer's views on astrobiology are in the first four paragraphs. He says that 'astrobiology is arguably the trendiest buzzword in science after genomics' (line 1). B is not possible because he asks, 'Is astrobiology a new name for repackaged goods (exobiology)?' (line 14) and answers 'No, for two reasons'. C states astrobiology 'has proved' the existence of fossils in a meteorite, whereas the text says these are 'much-disputed claims' (line 21). D contradicts the text, which says 'Significantly, Nature magazine recently looked at astrobiology in all its forms,' so a scientific publication took it seriously.

40 D

D correctly sums up the writer's main purpose overall. A is too general and vague. B deals only with part of the text near the start, not its main purpose. C gives an incorrect interpretation of what the text actually says.

Test 3

Listening

Section 1

Questions 1–6 page 74

Example   A
Lisa, in response to Dan's enquiry on 'what to bring with me', says 'most important of all are your documents', so these are essential.

1   A
The prompt comes when Lisa says 'let's start with cash'. She says 'make sure when you get here you have some cash on you,' specifying 'Pounds' and 'fifty, as an absolute minimum'.

2   A
Although Lisa says 'you will need warm clothing,' she then says 'you really don't need to bring much' as it can be bought cheaply nearby. However, she adds, 'Do make sure … that you have … a thick sweater and a jacket'.

3   C
Dan wonders 'whether to bring my computer,' and Lisa warns of incompatibility with the electricity supply and the risk of breakage. Dan asks about carrying it 'as hand luggage', but Lisa says this may not be possible, adding 'my advice is to leave yours at home.'

4   C
Dan asks: 'Is there anything else you'd advise against bringing?' Lisa first mentions items not included in the table ('household or cooking things'), but says later 'And importing food, of course, isn't allowed by Customs.'

5   B
Lisa introduces the answer by saying 'there one or two things I'd suggest you find room for in your suitcase,' and then suggests 'perhaps a few of your favourite cassettes or compact discs?' However, she does say 'you might be able to find them in the shops here,' reinforcing *recommended* rather than *essential*.

6   B
Lisa says 'some photographs of people and places that are special to you could be nice … It's just a thought,' which is a recommendation.

Questions 1–6: script

LISA Homestay Language Learning; Lisa McDowell here. How can I help you?

DAN Hello. My name's Dan…

LISA Hello Dan.

DAN and I'm going to be living with a family in Edinburgh for three months, so I'd like some advice on what to bring with me. I'm flying in via Singapore on the fifteenth.

LISA Right. Well perhaps most important of all are your documents: vaccination certificate, sponsor's letter and the certifying letter from us for Immigration.

DAN Yes, I've got all those in order, I think. What I'm really wondering about are money and clothes, and things for my room. Personal effects, in other words.

LISA OK, let's start with cash. You'll already have money in your bank account here, of course, but make sure when you get here you have some cash on you. Pounds that is, not euros or dollars.

DAN How much do you suggest?

LISA I'd say fifty, as an absolute minimum.

DAN OK. Now the next thing is which clothes to bring. What do think?

LISA Well, as I'm sure you know it can get pretty cold here, so you will need some warm clothing. There are shops near here that sell winter clothes quite cheaply, so you really don't need to bring much. Do make sure, though, that you have at least one thick sweater and a jacket with you when you arrive here: the temperature's likely to be a lot lower than in Singapore!

DAN Thanks for the warning! Now something else I'm not sure about is whether to bring my computer. It's a laptop, so it won't take up much room.

Lisa Two problems: firstly, it might not be compatible with the electricity supply in this country, and, secondly, there's a risk of it getting broken in transit. Someone travelling here had hers smashed only last month.

DAN But surely I can carry it as hand luggage?

LISA Usually, yes. But because of all the tight security right now you may have to check it in. So my advice is to leave yours at home.

DAN OK, I think I will. Is there anything else you'd advise against bringing?

LISA Well you won't need household or cooking things: they'll all be provided. And importing food, of course, isn't allowed by Customs. Though I imagine you already knew that.

DAN Well, er, yes.

LISA But there are one or two things I'd suggest you find room for in your suitcase…

DAN Yes?

LISA Perhaps a few of your favourite cassettes or compact disks? Of course, you might be able to find them in the shops here, but then again you might not.

DAN That's a good idea. Anything else?

LISA Yes - some photographs of people and places that are special to you could be nice. They can really make your room feel like home. It's just a thought.

DAN Hmm. I'll see if I've got a few good ones.

Questions 7–10 page 74

7 Wark
Lisa says 'make sure all your cases are clearly labelled, in English, with your host family's name and address'. Dan asks 'What name do I write' and Lisa replies 'Wark, Lewis and Amy Wark'. Dan says 'W-A-L-K' but Lisa corrects him: 'It's actually W-A-R-K'.

8 his hand luggage
Dan says 'I'd better put some essentials in my hand luggage', to which Lisa replies 'I'd recommend a change of T-shirt and socks and so on.'

9 wear tights
They both mention 'tights' before Dan gives the prompt 'for the flight'. He then refers to 'wearing them', and explains the health reasons: 'Wearing them helps prevent deep-vein thrombosis when you're flying long distances.'

10 500 metres
The prompt comes when Lisa says 'when you've packed your baggage.' She then says, 'check you can carry it – all of it – at least 500 metres.'

Questions 7–10: script

LISA Just a few points about packing: make sure all your cases are clearly labelled, in English, with your host family's name and address. Just in case they go missing on the way. It has been known to happen.

DAN What name do I write, by the way?

LISA It's 'Wark', Lewis and Amy Wark.

DAN So that's W-A-L-K?

LISA It's actually **W-A-R-K**, but we'll be posting full details to you later this week.

DAN Right, fine. And I'd better put some essentials in **my hand luggage**. Enough for a night or two in case, as you say, anything happens to my main, er, cases.

LISA Yes – I'd recommend a change of T-shirt and socks and so on, plus any medication you may need. And a toothbrush, of course.

DAN And my **tights**.

LISA Your **tights**?

DAN Yes, for the flight. Wearing them helps prevent deep-vein thrombosis when you're flying long distances, not getting any exercise.

LISA Oh yes … I've heard about that. Now talking about exercise, there's one last thing. When you've packed your baggage, check you can carry it – all of it – at least **500 metres**, without any help. You may have to do that!

DAN OK. Well, thanks for all your help. You've cleared up a lot of points.

LISA You're welcome. Have a safe journey, and we'll look forward to seeing you next month. Bye.

DAN Bye.

Section 2

Questions 11–13 page 75

11–13 A, C, F (any order)

A   Sally begins by saying 'although one in four people has some kind of disability, the proportion among students is much lower.' Option A is similar to this.

C   She says 'some (universities) have quite sticky problems' for wheelchair access caused by 'ancient buildings, cobbled streets built centuries ago, and so on.'

F   Referring to the disability advisor, she says 'often this person is a token … an extra responsibility given to a secretary. They don't know what the situation is in practice, and they don't have any real authority to change anything.'

Options not used

B   Although she mentions the age 25, and the fact that 'universities don't do much to encourage access,' she is referring to the disabled, not students over 25.

D   This may be a legal requirement in some countries, but it is not stated by Sally. She is talking about a document that explains university policy, not actual facilities.

E   This contradicts what she says: 'Most universities and some students' unions have a disability advisor.'

Questions 11–13: script

PRESENTER Welcome to Student Times, the programme with all the latest on what's happening at universities around the country. Today we'll be discussing disabled applicants, and the kind of support they can expect to find – or not find – at the university of their choice. With me to tell us more is Student Disability Advisor Sally Taylor. Good morning, Sally.

SALLY Good morning, Hugh. I'd like to start by pointing out that although one in four people has some kind of disability, the proportion among students is much lower. This is partly because most students are under 25 and many people only develop their disabilities as they get older - but it's also because some universities don't do much to encourage access. It is true, though, that some have quite sticky problems when it comes to, for instance, wheelchair access – ancient buildings, cobbled streets built centuries ago, and so on. When faced with such

a situation, some universities make an extra special effort to provide for students with particular disabilities, while others have specialist accommodation. In fact, all universities should have a written policy statement on students with disabilities, setting out what facilities they have, what their attitude is, and what they're prepared to do. But, having said that, only you can properly understand the challenges of any disability you have, and so, before accepting a place at a university (or even, while you're considering applying, if only to raise the universities' awareness), it's good to talk to them and find out how much they can (and will) do for you. The problem is who to talk to. Most universities and some students' unions have a disability advisor who is supposed to know what facilities they already have and will help with further arrangements if necessary or possible. However, all too often this person is a token. Sometimes it's just an extra responsibility given to a secretary. They don't know what the situation is in practice, and they don't have any real authority to change anything. So, given that for any prospective student it's best to visit a university before applying, it's an especially good idea for students with disabilities or special needs to check whether the place really does come up to scratch. In general, the university should provide personal care and assistance, and there are certain key features to look out for if you have a particular disability, including the following.

Questions 14–19   page 75

14   lifts that work
The prompt for the section is 'if your mobility is impaired,' and then 'fire and emergency procedures,' which precede the gap. The word 'lifts' alone is not sufficient: the speaker goes on to exclude 'the usual ones that seem to be out of order half the time.'

15   hearing impairment
Studying the preceding and following disabilities in the table should provide clues to the type of answer needed, and the first sentence of this section includes the words 'hearing impairment'.

16   visual doorbells
The flashing sirens above the gap provides a clue, and an explanation of what 'visual doorbells' actually do follows the use of the expression: they 'light up when somebody calls round to see you.'

17   clear markings
Following the reference to 'Braille translators', the parts of the buildings (stairs, floors, etc.) come before the mention of clear markings.

18   extra time
Answering this correctly requires you to understand reference words: in 'you should be allowed extra time to do so,' 'so' refers to completing exams, and in 'This applies to work in general too,' 'This' refers back to having extra time in the previous sentence.

19   emergency
After the mention of 'medication and/or therapy', Sally gives the answer: 'make sure that in the event of an emergency, it is clear what you – and other people who may be involved – have to do,' meaning the procedures you must follow.

Question 20   page 76

20   D
B is correct because it reflects the advisory content and tone of the text, which addresses the reader as 'you'. A relates only to the beginning of the text. C is wrong because there is no mention of a specific university (one aim of the text is to enable disabled students to make an informed choice of university). D is incorrect because, although there is general criticism of

universities at the beginning, including criticism of the lack of effective disability officers, it is balanced with some explanation and praise. There is no real criticism of facilities, so this cannot be the main purpose.

Questions 14–20: script

SALLY Firstly, if your mobility is impaired, check there are ramps and easy access to all buildings, not just accommodation or teaching rooms. Then, when you're inside, look for clear instructions on fire and emergency procedures for the disabled. Also make sure there are **lifts that work** – not the usual ones that seem to be out of order half the time – and check for suitable lavatory facilities. There is a different set of things to look for if you suffer from any kind of **hearing impairment**. There should be induction loops in lecture theatres, flashing sirens in all rooms, and, in accommodation, **visual doorbells** that light up when somebody calls round to see you. If it is your sight that is impaired, there obviously need to be Braille translators of books and documents. In all buildings, the stairs, floors, doorways and windows must have **clear markings**, and there also have to be special fire and emergency procedures for you. If you suffer from dyslexia, you will need a computer for general use and in exams. And, as exams may take you longer to complete, you should be allowed **extra time** in which to do so. This applies to work in general, too. There are of course many other possible health difficulties that you may suffer from, such as diabetes, epilepsy, or heart conditions. If this is the case, check the availability of access to appropriate treatment including medication and/or therapy. Finally, make sure that in the event of an **emergency**, it is clear what you – and other people who may be involved – have to do.

Section 3

Questions 21–26 page 76

21 C
Liz says 'one of the most useful things was chatting to people who'd already been there for a year, so-called senior students.'

22 B
Liz describes 'the great atmosphere at the formal dinner', saying 'it was one of the high points of the whole week.'

23 F
The prompt comes when Liz says 'they took us round the city centre'. After Mark's comment, she says 'it was very worthwhile.'

24 E
Mark says 'maybe they could have taken us to a better night club. The music at the place we went to was lousy.'

25 A
Liz says 'they showed us round everything on the campus', prompting Mark to complain 'it *was* everything … I could have done with less information on every building,' suggesting there should have been 'more on places everyone's likely to use … .'

26 D
Liz talks of 'an afternoon session on how to drive in this country'. Mark says 'I was a bit disappointed,' and 'it might have been more helpful if it had included stuff for pedestrians.'

Questions 21–26: script

JULIA So you were both on last year's Orientation Course, then. How did it go?

LIZ I loved it. The activities were well organized, and I met people from all over the world.

MARK Yes, it was useful.

JULIA And you think I should sign up for this year's course?

LIZ Yes, definitely. Apart from being fun, it really does prepare you for all the things you have to do in your first couple of weeks. In fact, one of the most useful things was chatting to people who'd already been there for a year, so-called senior students. They'd been on the Orientation Course the year before last, and recommended it to us. Oh, and there was a great atmosphere at the formal dinner, too. It was so colourful, with people in their traditional dress from Asia, Africa, South America. It was one of the high points of the whole week.

MARK That was right at the end, of course. The first thing they did, on the Monday, was take us on a guided tour of the Students Union.

LIZ And after that they took us round the city centre, showing us things like the bus station, the main shops …

MARK And the best pubs …

LIZ Right. So it was very worthwhile.

MARK Yes, though maybe they could have taken us to a better night club. The music at the place we went to was lousy.

LIZ That's a matter of taste, surely! Well anyway the next day they showed us round everything on the campus.

MARK And believe me it was everything. We must have walked miles. I could have done with less information on every building in sight, given that I'll probably never need to go into half of them, and a bit more on places everyone's likely to use at some time or other. Like the sports block, the health centre, the bicycle and car parks …

LIZ Which reminds me, there was an afternoon session on how to drive in this country, which seemed to me a bit weird – you know, for a university course.

MARK I suppose it's because there've been accidents involving students who aren't used to people driving on the left. I was there actually.

LIZ How was it?

MARK Well, I must say I was a bit disappointed. There were some useful driving tips, but it might have been more helpful if it had included stuff for pedestrians. How to avoid getting run over, for example.

LIZ You didn't go to the session on 'safety', then?

MARK No.

LIZ Well apparently that dealt with road safety for pedestrians, along with lots of other aspects of course. I wasn't there myself, but that might be something worth going to, Julia.

Questions 27–30 page 77

27 D

The prompt is from Julia: 'what's the accommodation like?' Mark says 'The room will have chairs, table, wardrobe, bed, mattress, blankets, sheets,' so D is right. A is wrong because Julia asks 'Do you have a room to yourself or do you have to share?', to which Liz replies 'You'll have an individual room.' B isn't possible because Liz says the room 'will be in a different hall from the one you're booked into for the year.' C isn't possible because Liz says the rooms 'are both on the campus so you won't have far to go.'

28 B

Liz says 'it's unlikely to reach even twenty degrees', so it cannot be either C or D. Mark's point 'it shouldn't drop below about ten, at least during the day ', means that A is not possible, so taking Liz and Mark's comments together gives the answer B.

29 B

The prompt comes when Liz says 'they gave us free email access.' Mark says 'I think it was twenty', which Liz confirms by saying 'Yes, you're right.' A is wrong because Liz's first statement 'thirty minutes, if I remember correctly' is incorrect. C and D are also wrong: Liz mentions 'ten' and 'fifteen' minutes in relation to the extra time she paid for, not free email time.

30 C

Julia asks 'When does the course actually start and finish?' Mark says Monday is 'when things get going.' Julia asks 'And that's it, is it?' and Liz confirms, 'Yes, there's nothing after that.' Although Mark says 'a lot of people get there on the Sunday,' this is not when the activities begin. A and B are therefore wrong. Mark does say 'most people stay over till Saturday,' but not for activities, so D is wrong.

Questions 27–30: script

JULIA I like the sound of the whole thing. Tell me, what's the accommodation like? Do you have a room to yourself or do you have to share? What do you have to take with you?

LIZ For the orientation course, you'll have an individual room in one of the halls of residence. That'll be a different hall from the one you're booked into for the year, but they're both on the campus so you won't have far to go.

MARK And you won't have to take too much with you. The room will have chairs, table, wardrobe, bed, mattress, blankets, sheets and so on.

LIZ Take a warm coat or jacket, though. It may well rain and it's unlikely to reach even twenty degrees in late September.

MARK But it shouldn't drop below about ten, at least during the day. Which is something, I suppose!

JULIA Right. Now I know they can't do much about the weather, but did you have the feeling that they were looking after you on the course?

LIZ Yes, we did. There were some little touches that showed they'd thought about what it was like to be starting a course of study abroad.

JULIA Such as?

LIZ Well it's just a small example, but they gave us free email access to contact people at home. Thirty minutes, if I remember correctly.

MARK Actually I think it was twenty.

LIZ Yes, you're right. I was on for over half an hour and paid for an extra ten or fifteen minutes. Not that it was much!

JULIA Emails don't take long to write anyway.

LIZ No, they don't.

JULIA So, just one more thing: the timetable. When does the course actually start and finish?

MARK Well a lot of people get there on the Sunday, though you'd have to find a room for an extra night as the course accommodation is only booked from the Monday, when things get going.

LIZ Then they'll keep you busy all week, until the dinner on the Friday.

JULIA And that's it, is it?

LIZ Yes, there's nothing after that.

MARK Though most people stay over till Saturday, partly to recover from the party but also because they can then move straight into their permanent rooms.

JULIA I think I'll do that. Well, thanks a lot for all your advice. I'm sure I'll enjoy the course.

LIZ I wish I could go on this year's, too!

Section 4

Questions 31–33 page 78

31 sixth/6th
The lecturer speaks of 'disagreement as to exactly when, or even in which century', before stating 'the consensus nowadays, though, is that it was in the *sixth*'.

32 Chinese Arrows
The speaker says 'fireworks were in use by the seventh century in Arabia, where they were called "*Chinese Arrows*"," with the 'military' reference helping to confirm 'arrows'.

33 Europe
The speaker says 'It took a long time for them to spread to *Europe*: in fact it wasn't until the twelve hundreds that fireworks made their appearance there.'

Questions 31–33: script

LECTURER Good afternoon everyone, and welcome to this short talk on the subject of fireworks. Now, fireworks, as I'm sure many of you know, were invented in China, though there has long been disagreement as to exactly when, or even in which century. The consensus nowadays, though, is that it was in the **sixth**, as there is considerable evidence of war rockets being made then. We also know that fireworks were in use by the seventh century in Arabia, where they were called '**Chinese Arrows**', reflecting their military potential. It then took a long time for them to spread to **Europe**: in fact it wasn't until the twelve hundreds that fireworks made their appearance there.

Questions 34–37 page 78

34 shell
The speaker says a *shell* is 'often a sphere about the size of a peach', which describes 34 in the diagram.

35 75/seventy-five mm/millimetres
The reference to the 'mortar' comes after the answer. The speaker says 'a shell of this kind is launched from a *75 millimetre* diameter mortar.' Here diameter means width.

36 500/five hundred mm/millimetres
The speaker refers to the mortar as a 'steel or … shatterproof plastic pipe'. The next sentence refers back to the pipe: 'this is likely to be *500 millimetres* long.'

37 lifting
There is a description which matches the diagram: 'at the bottom of the pipe, below the shell, is placed a cylinder containing black powder. This has a long fuse which projects out of the tube.' Then comes the answer: 'when this is lit, it quickly burns down to the *lifting charge*.'

Questions 38–40 page 79

38 B
B is correct: the text says 'some shells contain explosives designed to crackle in the sky, or whistles that explode outwards'. A is wrong because there is no mention of danger, despite the use of words such as 'explode' and 'bursting'. C contradicts the speaker: 'the sections of a multibreak shell are ignited by different fuses.'

39 C
C is correct because the speaker says 'to create a specific figure in the sky, for instance a heart shape, you create an outline of the figure in stars'. A is incorrect because the speaker says 'if the stars are equally spaced in a circle … you will see … explosions equally spaced in a circle,' not a heart. B is also incorrect: there is no suggestion that the stars themselves are 'heart-shaped'.

40 B
B matches the description of 'The Serpentine (which) sends small tubes of incendiaries scattering outwards in random paths, which may culminate in exploding stars'. A matches 'the Ring Shell (which) is produced by stars exploding outwards to produce a symmetrical ring'. C matches the Palm which 'contains large comets, or charges … these travel outwards, explode and then curve downwards like the limbs of a palm tree.'

Questions 34–40: script

LECTURER The basic ingredients of fireworks have changed little to this day. Their explosive capacity comes mainly from black powder, also known as gunpowder, which is produced from a mixture of charcoal, sulphur and potassium nitrate. A modern aerial firework – the kind used nowadays in big public displays, not the small rocket type that you might remember from your childhood - is normally made in the form of a **shell**, often a sphere about the size of a peach. Inside the shell are a number of stars surrounded by black powder, and running through the centre of the round shell is a charge that makes the firework explode when it reaches the desired altitude. This is known as the bursting charge. When this explodes, it ignites the outside of the stars, which begin to burn with bright showers of sparks. Since the explosion throws the stars in all directions, you get the huge sphere of sparkling light that is so familiar at firework displays. A shell of this kind is launched from a **75 millimetre**-diameter mortar, which in some ways resembles the type used by the military. The mortar is a steel or – increasingly, for safety reasons – shatterproof plastic pipe. This is likely to be **500 millimetres** long and sealed at one end. The other end is aimed at the sky and at the bottom of the pipe, below the shell, is placed a cylinder containing black powder. This has a long fuse which projects out of the tube. When this is lit, it quickly burns down to the **lifting** charge, which explodes to launch the shell. In so doing, it also lights the shell's fuse. The shell's fuse burns while the shell rises to its correct altitude, and then ignites the bursting charge so it explodes. More complicated shells are divided into sections and burst in two or three phases. Shells like this are called multibreak shells. They may contain stars of different colours and compositions to create softer or brighter light, more or less sparks, etc. Some shells contain explosives designed to crackle in the sky, or whistles that explode outwards with the stars. The sections of a multibreak shell are ignited by different fuses and the bursting of one section ignites the next. The shells must be assembled in such a way that each section explodes in sequence to produce a distinct separate effect. The pattern that an aerial shell paints in the sky depends on the arrangement of stars inside the shell. For example, if the stars are equally spaced in a circle, with black powder inside the circle, you will see an aerial display of smaller star explosions equally spaced in a circle. To create a specific figure in the sky, for instance a heart shape, you create an outline of the figure in stars inside the shell. You then place explosive charges inside those stars to blow them outward into the shape of a large heart. Each charge has to be ignited at exactly the right time or the whole thing is spoiled. Many other shapes have particular names, like the Willow. This is formed by stars that fall in the shape of willow tree branches spreading a little to the side and then downwards. The high charcoal composition of the stars makes them long-burning, so they may even stay visible until they hit the ground. The Ring Shell is fairly basic. It is produced by stars exploding outwards to produce a symmetrical ring of coloured lights. More complex is the pattern created by the Palm, which contains large comets, or charges in the shape of a solid cylinder. These travel outwards, explode and then curve downwards like the limbs of a palm tree. The Serpentine, the last one for now, is different again. When this one bursts, it sends small tubes of incendiaries scattering outwards in random paths, which may culminate in exploding stars. It can be quite spectacular.

Academic reading

Passage 1

Questions 1–4 page 82

1 B
The long synonym for skin – 'this impervious yet permeable barrier' – is followed by 'is composed of three layers.' Clues include 'outermost' and 'epidermis' (on ... the surface), as well as the 'dermis' and 'innermost layer' (below the surface).

2 H
There are two experiments in this paragraph. The neuroscientist tells the writer 'Open your eyes' *after* the first experiment. In the second, the writer says he has 'visual proof': he can see what is happening.

3 J
The writer addresses the reader directly – 'If you ever touch a hot burner' – and uses the imperative to indicate advice – 'just put your finger in cold water.' The physical results of this ('no blister ... no scar') are that damage will be avoided.

4 D
The first sentence of D mentions 'experiments decades ago, now considered unethical and inhumane,' in which they 'kept baby monkeys from being touched by their mothers.'

Questions 5 and 6 page 82

5 B
The relevant paragraph is E ('insufficient touching in early years can have lifelong results' corresponds to the question), and the beginning of paragraph F. There are two clues which confirm B: 'where touch is limited, adult aggression is high', and the correlation of 'high rates of physical affection in childhood with low rates of adult physical violence.' A takes the word 'apathetic' from the text, but there it is used about monkeys. C contradicts the text, and also implies a change in behaviour as children become adults that is not stated in the text. D is contradicted by the first clause of paragraph F: 'the effects of touching are easy to understand.'

6 C
C is confirmed when the writer admits 'my skin ... has been deceiving me my entire life,' and that 'my skin feels pressure and temperature (but) it's my brain that says I feel wet.' A is incorrect because the writer does not suggest there is anything wrong with his skin, or that it is in any way unusual. B is incorrect since in paragraphs G and H the neuroscientist explains that the skin cannot feel 'wetness', only 'pressure, pain and temperature'. D is incorrect since, in addition to the above, the writer admits his mistake by saying 'I now realize ...'

Questions 7–11 page 83

7 E
Earlier in paragraph C, the writer states 'We can live without seeing or hearing – in fact, without any of our other senses' so E is correct. The fact that option E will not fit any of the other answers grammatically helps to confirm this. Option J looks possible but is incorrect since paragraph C refers to some 'babies born without effective nerve connections between skin and brain.'

8 H
The writer twice explains why a substance feels wet in paragraph H: 'The combination of pressure and cold ... is what makes my skin perceive wetness,' and 'my skin feels pressure and temperature. It's my brain that says I feel wet.' You need to be careful with other sensations, and the combination of cold and pain in option A – pain is not mentioned in relation to wetness.

9 D
Paragraph I paraphrases question 8 and option D together: '.' Don't be misled by the reference in option C to the skin being thin – this has no connection with ticklishness.

10 G
The answer to this follows the answer to question 8 in paragraph I: 'Gentle stimulation of pressure receptors can result in ticklishness; gentle stimulation of pain receptors in itching.'

11 B
Paragraph J explains how a small cut – 'I nicked myself with a knife' – heals up quickly – 'It's only been a few days but my little self-repair is almost complete.' This is because 'epidermal cells are

migrating into the wound to close it up', i.e. it can mend itself. Paragraph B had explained that the epidermis is the outer layer.

Questions 12–14 page 83

12 True
The beginning of paragraph F states 'the effects of touching are easy to understand', in contrast with 'the mechanics of it' – in other words, how our sense of touch works. That even scientists find it difficult is shown when Bolanowski, a neuroscientist, says 'no one knows exactly how it takes place.'

13 Not given
Although 'pressure' is mentioned more often than 'temperature' or 'pain' in the examples given, there is no suggestion that this is because the skin is any more sensitive to this stimulus than to the other two.

14 False
The first indication that the statement is false is 'Repairs occur with varying success.' Although the writer says 'my little self-repair is now complete … we recover quickly from slight burns, these are minor injuries', this contrasts with the final sentence: 'Severe burns, though, are a different matter.'

Passage 2

Questions 15–19 page 84

15 Section A: viii
The first section focuses on 'locksmiths', who open locks legally, and 'burglars', who don't, as well as 'spies', 'detectives', and the 'determined intruder'.

16 Section B: vii
Section A outlines the connection between key, lock and bolt, using the example of the dead-bolt.

17 Section C: ix
This section mainly describes the workings of a pin lock, which, as pointed out at the beginning of the second paragraph, is a kind of cylinder lock.

18 Section D: ii
This section explains the use of lock-picking tools to open a lock.

19 Section E: vi
As well as adding more information about pin locks, this section also introduces two other kinds of lock: 'wafer' and 'tubular'.

Headings not used
i   There is no discussion of this anywhere in the text. Although Section E describes the more secure 'tubular lock', it says they are used on 'vending machines'.
iii Section D mentions two types of tool, but there is no advice on which to choose, or how.
iv   This is the topic only of the first paragraph in Section C.
v   How to open a lock with a different key is not discussed in any of the sections.
x   The technique of picking only one kind of lock (pin) is explained in Section D. Although E mentions the relative difficulty of picking different kinds, it doesn't explain how to do so.

Questions 20–22 page 86

20 housing
This is described in Section C as 'the outer part of the lock which does not move', with further references such as 'vertical shafts that run down from the *housing*'.

21 cylinder
The overview of the system at the beginning of C explains the role of the *cylinder*: 'the key turns a *cylinder* in the middle of the lock.' The next two paragraphs confirm the position of 'the central *cylinder*', referring to 'shafts that run down from the housing into the *cylinder*.'

22 pins
The second paragraph in C explains what and where they are: 'Inside these shafts are pairs of metal *pins* of varying length, held in position by small springs.' There are more references in the next paragraph.

Questions 23–25 page 87

23 (a/the) (tension) wrench
The words that explain this are 'insert *the tension wrench* into the keyhole and turn it … This turns the cylinder so that it is slightly offset from the housing around it'.

24 (a/the) pick
The text says 'While applying pressure on the cylinder, slide the *pick* into the keyhole.'

25 (the) ledge (in shaft)
The text has mentioned 'a slight *ledge* in the pin shafts', and now says 'The *ledge* keeps the upper pin wedged in the housing, so it won't fall back into the cylinder.' This ledge is maintained by 'applying pressure with the tension wrench.'

Questions 26–27 page 87

26 moderate security
The beginning of section E says these locks 'offer moderate security'. Notice the similarity in meaning to *relatively low security* above, and in form (adjective + noun) to the one below that: *superior protection*.

27 wafer
The second paragraph of section E deals with this type of lock. The clues 'relatively low security' and 'most cars' are in the last sentence.

Passage 3

Questions 28–31 page 90

28 Yes
The text says the outcome of 'many mergers and acquisitions, strategic alliances and joint ventures between British and European companies is that they do not achieve their objectives and end in tears' (lines 18–21), i.e. they often fail.

29 Yes
The text states that 'The result is a management culture which is … focused almost entirely on the short term' (lines 56–58). This is referring back to the objectives of 'project management principles' (line 45).

30 No
In lines 68–70, the writer says, 'in flattened and decentralised' (i.e. segmented) 'organisations, there are very limited career prospects.'

31 No
This is contradicted in lines 88–94: 'European organizations continue to be structured hierarchically … with explicit channels of reporting … Decision making…remains essentially top-down' (i.e. orders come from above).

Questions 32–37 page 90

32 increasing
The references in the text to a 'long-hours working culture' (line 98) and 'excessively long working hours' (lines 108–109) make *increasing* correct and the alternative adjective *declining* clearly wrong.

33 reach
A verb is needed here, so it is a choice between *reach* and *predict*. The first of these more accurately reflects the text reference 'if the targets are to be achieved' (lines 108–109).

34 agreement
The nouns with similar meanings are *argument*, *agreement* and *discussion*. The text mentions 'ongoing dispute' (line 112) and 'objections' (line 113) in relation to measures of performance. However, the negative 'nor' in the summary makes *argument* or *discussion* impossible.

35 manufacturing
The two adjectives likely to fit are *manufacturing* and *office*. The contrast in the text is between activities in 'labs', 'offices', and 'marketing departments' on the one hand, and 'a factory producing cars' on the other (lines 117–122). The answer must be *manufacturing*. Also, *clerical* means *office* in this context, so the alternative would not make sense.

36 pressure
The possible nouns are *pressure* and *temperature*. Don't be misled by the apparent similarity of the latter to 'burn-out' in the text (line 126): there is no connection in meaning.

37 unwilling

The choice of three nouns – *willing, able* and *unwilling* – makes complete understanding of the text essential. The verb form 'would work' indicates willingness (not ability) to continue working to 65, but as the figures have been reversed to give a negative perspective (80% as opposed to 'a fifth' in the text), the answer too must be negative.

Questions 38–39 page 91

38 family-friendly

Lines 133–135 state 'the European management model allows for family-friendly employment policies,' and although the text says this may also be the case where project management principles operate, it specifies 'in theory' and then goes to suggest what happens in practice.

39 (annual) leave

The idea of *tight deadlines* is contained in the lines 143–147: 'the business plan has to be finished by the end of the month, the advertising campaign completed by the end of next week … to achieve measurable targets.' The writer than asks the rhetorical question about 'taking our full annual leave'.

Question 40 page 91

40 B

After criticizing the effects of the American model in the UK and comparing it with the European, the writer asks 'Which of these two models is preferable?' (line 195) and then gives arguments in favour of the European one for Britain. A incorrectly interprets what the writer says, and also deals with only an incidental point. C is beyond the scope of the text: no new model is put forward, just a choice between two existing ones. D is not the 'main purpose' of the text. Although the topic is mentioned in several paragraphs, it is as an example from only one sector of the economy.

Test 4

Listening

Section 1

Questions 1–4 page 98

1 driving licence
After the prompt 'pieces of identity', Terry mentions 'a valid passport' and says 'the next one is a driving licence, and again one from your country would be OK'.

2 benefit book
Terry reads out 'a birth certificate', but this cannot be used as Sam is not under 18. He then suggests 'a benefit book', and she replies, 'Yes, could bring that'. She asks about 'a letter from your employer', but Terry says, 'that's not actually on the list, so we'll have to assume you can't.'

3 insurance certificate
Sam asks what she can use 'to prove where I live', and Terry mentions 'a bill for council tax', and just after that 'an insurance certificate'. Sam says 'I've got one of those.'

4 electricity bill
Sam asks about 'a bill for my mobile', but Terry says 'I'm afraid it would have to be for a fixed line phone.' She then suggests 'an electricity bill' and Terry indicates she could use that 'if it's in your name', to which she replies, 'It is.'

Questions 5–7 page 98

5 9.30–3.30
Following Sam's question about 'their business hours', Terry talks of 'a change at some banks in the last year or so', so 9.00 until 4.00 is wrong. He then says it is 'open from nine thirty in the morning till half past three in the afternoon.'

6 ground floor
Sam asks for confirmation that 'it's on the top floor of the Centre building,' to which Terry replies, 'That's where it used to be,' i.e. it is no longer there. He goes on to say 'it's on the ground floor now.'

7 no / nothing
After mentioning 'incentives…to open accounts,' Sam asks 'if they are offering anything,' and Terry replies, 'I'm sure they'd say so on their "new clients" page if they were,' and then 'no, there's nothing mentioned there.' Terry then mentions a 'free gift'.

Questions 1–7: script

TERRY Expats Helpline; Terry Davies here. What can I do for you?

SAM Hello Terry, I've been in this country for a while and I've just been offered a job in the city, so I think I'm going to need to open a bank account. I haven't had one before, so I'm wondering what papers I need.

TERRY Well basically you'll need to be able to prove to the bank that you're who you say you are and that you live where you say you do, OK?

SAM Uh-huh.

TERRY And for some banks, at least, that means you'll have to show them two separate pieces of identity, so I'll run through the list if you like.

SAM Yes, please.

TERRY OK, I'll bring it up on the screen. Let's see … here it is … right, the first thing it says is 'a valid passport'.

SAM Mine's Australian.

TERRY Yes, that would be fine of course. The next one is 'a **driving licence**', and again one from your country would be OK. Then that's followed by 'birth certificate'… oh hang on, that's only if you're under 18.

SAM Which I'm not.

TERRY Right, so not that then. But you can also show them a '**benefit book**', for instance if you're in ill-health or unemployed or getting income support.

SAM Yes, I could bring that. Or a letter from my employer, maybe?

TERRY Well that's not actually on the list; so we'll have to assume you can't.

SAM OK. And to prove where I live?

TERRY Again, there are several possible things listed here. For instance you could use a bill for council tax, or something else for where you live, such as an **insurance certificate**.

SAM I've got one of those. Somewhere among all my papers. But what about bills? Things like phone bills, I mean.

TERRY As long as it has your address on it, yes, fine.

SAM So a bill for my mobile would do, would it?

TERRY Ah - I'm afraid it would have to be for a fixed line phone. You could use other types of household bill, though. As long as you get them through the post.

SAM How about an **electricity bill**? That'll say where I live, won't it?

TERRY If it's in your name, and not that of a er … landlord, yes.

SAM It is, so I'll probably take that then.

TERRY There's one other you might want to use: a 'vehicle registration document'. If you have a car or motorbike or something, of course.

SAM No I haven't, actually.

SAM Now I believe there's a bank actually inside the Commercial Centre, and I might open an account there, seeing as how that's where I'll be every day.

TERRY Yes, that would seem to make sense. I know people who bank there.

SAM I actually read about it in a city guide – my cousin picked it up when he was here a couple of years ago – and I made a few notes. Do you mind if I run through them with you now, just to make sure the details haven't changed?

TERRY Fine – go ahead.

SAM OK, first question: it's still a branch of the Popular Bank, is it, the one with links to Australian banks?

TERRY No, it's actually been taken over by another big banking group: the Savings Bank. It still seems quite popular, though, especially with people doing business in the Asia/Pacific area.

SAM And when is it open? Monday to Saturday?

TERRY I'll have to check their website for that. Give me a second or two, will you.

SAM Sure.

TERRY Right, I've got it … 'customer service' … and it's … just weekdays, I'm afraid.

SAM Does it say what their business hours are?

TERRY I'm just looking for that, it's on a different page for some reason … I think there's been a change at some banks in the last year or so … yes here it is … it's open from **nine thirty** in the morning till **half past three** in the afternoon.

SAM And it's on the top floor of the main Centre building is it, next to the Travel Agency?

TERRY That's where it used to be, but they've since moved it to a slightly bigger place. It's on the **ground floor** now.

SAM And one last thing on this: I know most banks give incentives to young people to open accounts with them, but apparently this one didn't. Do you know if they are offering anything these days?

TERRY I'll just check … I'm sure they'd say so on their 'new clients' page if they were … no, there's **nothing** mentioned there.

SAM That's a pity. I was quite looking forward to getting my free gift!

Questions 8–10 page 99

8 F
Terry says 'turn left' from the Centre, going past the 'Post Office', and then 'turn left up Bridge Street' past the 'Shaw Theatre' and 'take the first right'. The Royal Bank is 'on the right, directly opposite the Park Hotel' (not the Internet café).

9 A
After turning 'right' from the Centre and going 'along Market Street' until 'the junction with West Street', the advice is to 'turn right again', and 'carry on up as far as the next junction, where you take a left.' After crossing the road and turning left, the bank is 'the third building on the right' (not B, the first).

10 C
Sam can go 'either way from the Centre: up West Street or Bridge Street and then along past the City Hall'. The bank is 'on the other side of the road, right next to the Tourist Office', so it must be C, not D.

Questions 8–10: script

TERRY There are plenty of other banks within walking distance you know. It may be worth shopping around to see what they've got to offer: longer opening hours, including Saturdays, perhaps less crowded …

SAM Can you tell me how to get to a couple of them? I know where the Commercial Centre is, so that's probably my best starting place.

TERRY Sure. For the Royal Bank you need to turn left when you leave the Centre, go along Market Street past the Post Office, and turn left up Bridge Street, past the Shaw Theatre. Then you take the first right. You'll see an Internet café on the other side and the Royal is just a bit further along on the right, directly opposite the Park Hotel.

SAM OK, I've got that. What about the Northern Bank?

TERRY For that one you turn right as you come out of the Centre, and go along Market Street until you come to the junction with West Street. There you turn right again, and carry on up as far as the next junction, where you take a left. You'll see the bank from there: it's the third building on the right.

SAM Fine. And the last one, the National Bank?

TERRY You can go either way from the Centre, really: up West Street or Bridge Street and then along past City Hall. The bank is on the other side of the road, right next to the Tourist Office. You can't miss it.

SAM Great. Thanks a lot for you help.

TERRY Any time. Bye.

SAM Bye

Section 2

Questions 11–14 page 100

11 work samples
Following the prompt for Step 1 'preparation is a key to success,' and the reference to the first point 'begin by collecting together all the documents,' the speaker gives the answer, adding 'you could also take some *work samples*, selecting from what you have designed, drawn, or written, for instance'.

12 job description
Sandy introduces Step 2 by stating that 'the more you know … the better prepared you will be', before advising 'request a *job description* from the employer'.

13 employees
After referring to the Chamber of Commerce and library, they suggest 'network with people who work for the company, or *employees* of companies associated with it'.

14 experience or skills
The speaker mentions 'the next step' and the advice is to 'match your qualifications to the requirements,' then 'think about some standard interview questions and how you might respond,' and finally 'if you don't have any *experience or skills* … think about how you might compensate'.

Questions 11–14: script

PRESENTER Today I have with me Sandy Richardson of the local Workforce Center, and she'll be talking about that critical step towards the goal of employment: the interview. Sandy, what is an interview for, and what's the best way to approach it?

SANDY A job interview is simply a meeting between you and a potential employer to discuss your qualifications and see if there is a 'fit'. The employer wants to verify what they know about you and talk about your qualifications. If you have been called for an interview, you can assume that the employer is interested in you. The employer has a need that you may be able to meet, so it's your goal to identify that need and convince the employer that you're the one for the job. As everyone knows, interviews can be stressful, but when you're well prepared there's no reason to panic. Preparation is the key to success in a job search, and you can begin by collecting together all the documents you may need for the interview, such as extra copies of your resumé, lists of references, and letters of recommendation. You could also take some **work samples**, selecting from what you have designed, drawn or written, for instance. And make sure you have a pen and pad of paper for taking notes. The next step is to find out about the post. The more you know about the job, the employer and the industry, the better prepared you will be to target your qualifications. Always request a **job description** from the employer, and research employer profiles at the Chamber of Commerce or local library. You could also try to network with people who work for the company, or with **employees** of companies associated with it. The next step is to match your qualifications to the requirements of the job. A good approach is to write out your qualifications along with the job requirements. Think about some standard interview questions and how you might respond. Most questions are designed to find out more about you, your qualifications or to test your reactions in a given situation. If you don't have any **experience or skills** in a required area, think about how you might compensate for those deficiencies.

Questions 15–20 page 100

15 ten minutes
Don't be misled by the reference to '30 seconds': that contrasts with 'plenty of time'. The advice is not to arrive 'too early', in other words '*10 minutes* at most'.

16 take your time

Sandy recommends you should 'listen carefully to each question' and then '*take your time* in responding'.

17 ask for clarification

The prompt is 'if you are unsure of a question', followed by the answer in 'don't be afraid to *ask for clarification*.'

18 salary

The prompt comes in the reference to 'your *salary* requirements', followed by the clue 'avoid the question until you have been offered the job'. The answer is heard again in the warning about 'questions about *salary* asked before there is a job offer'.

19 confident

First there is a clue: 'the more you learn from the experience, the easier the next one will become.' This is followed by the reason: 'You'll become much more *confident*.'

20 appearance

The speaker gives examples of changes to appearance, such as clothing, visiting the hairdresser's, and having a shave. Then the speaker paraphrases the given sentence: 'Remember that your *appearance* is a key indicator of whether you have the right attitude, so it can pay to give some thought to how you look.'

Questions 15–20: script

Sandy   During an interview it's important that you be yourself. Get a good night's sleep and plan your travel to be there in plenty of time, so that you're not arriving out of breath with 30 seconds to spare. Don't, though, present yourself for the interview too early: **ten minutes** at most. In the interview, listen carefully to each question asked. **Take your time** in responding and make sure your answers are positive. It's important to express a good attitude and show that you are willing to work, eager to learn and are flexible. If you are unsure of a question, don't be afraid to **ask for clarification**. In fact, it's sometimes a good strategy is to close a response with a question for the interviewer. In general, focus on your qualifications and look for opportunities to personalize the interview. Briefly answer questions with examples of how you responded in comparable situations, from either your life or previous job experiences. Something you should avoid are 'yes' or 'no' responses to questions, but don't dwell too long on non-job related topics. Use caution if you are questioned about your **salary** requirements. The best strategy is to avoid the question until you have been offered a job. Questions about **salary** asked before there is a job offer are usually screening questions that may eliminate you from consideration, so be warned. On the other hand, it isn't inappropriate to show your enthusiasm if your first impressions of the interview and of the employer are good ones, so, if the job sounds like what you are looking for - say so. Keep in mind that the interview is not over when you are asked if you have any questions. Come prepared to ask a couple of specific questions that again show your knowledge and interest in the job. Close the interview in the same friendly, positive manner in which you started. When the interview is over, leave promptly. Don't overstay your time. Think about the interview and learn from the experience. Evaluate the success and failures. The more you learn from the interview, the easier the next one will become. You'll become much more **confident**. To close, here are a few more tips. First, maintain good eye contact throughout the interview, and be aware of nonverbal body language. Second, dress a step above what you would wear on the job, go to the hairdresser's, have a shave, et cetera. Remember that your **appearance** is a key indicator of whether you have the right attitude, so it can pay to give some thought to how you look. And, finally, don't be a clock watcher!

Section 3

Questions 21–24 page 101

21 university
The speaker says that 'employers will be at least as interested in how well a student has performed academically, and how the whole experience of *university* has developed the student as a person.'

22 interesting
The tutor suggests 'selecting modules that will interest you' and 'in which you think you will be particularly successful.'

23 vocational
The tutor says 'on certain degree courses … module choice can be important. This applies mainly to *vocational* courses.'

24 careers service
The prompt is 'academic department' and a further clue is 'anything you're not certain about,' which comes after the answer. The alternative to the 'academic department' on the recording is 'the university's *Careers Service*'.

Questions 21–24: script

TUTOR As you know, this week you choose your modules for the first year of study, so this introductory meeting is aimed at helping you make informed choices. I think the best way to do this is on a question-and-answer basis, so who'd like to start? Pat?

PAT Yes, there's something I've been wondering about: will my choice affect my career opportunities?

TUTOR Well, for most students the choice of Level One modules won't be crucial in terms of a later career. In fact, many graduate level jobs will accept graduates from a range of degree courses. Employers will often be at least as interested in how well a student has performed academically, and how the whole experience of **university** has developed the student as a person, as in the detail of the course options chosen. Selecting modules that will **interest** you and in which you think you will be particularly successful is therefore also likely to make good sense in career terms. On certain degree courses, though, module choice can be important. This applies mainly to **vocational** courses where the degree confers an accredited professional training as well as university

education. Usually the modules students are required to take will include all those needed to meet those professional requirements. Your academic department, in this case Chemical and Process Engineering, and the university's **Careers Service** will be able to advise you, and will be pleased to help you sort out anything you're not certain about.

PAT Right.

Questions 25–29 page 101

25 A
Rajav is talking about Applied Chemical Engineering when he asks about 'the Information Technology part of the module', and the tutor's reply mentions 'word processing' and 'spreadsheets.'

26 C
Pat's question refers to 'Science 1 in Chemical Engineering', and the tutor explains: 'students who have already studied physics are excused the physics lectures, while those who've done biology are exempt from attending the biology lectures.'

27 B
When Sonia asks 'how is that module (Fluid Mechanics) tested?', the tutor says 'That's one of those which still uses written exams. The sit-down, formal type.'

28 A
Referring to the topics covered in Applied Chemical Engineering, the tutor mentions 'interviewing techniques, presentation skills, and producing written reports'.

29 C
Pat asks about 'the teaching approach', and the tutor says 'you are encouraged to learn by working out the solutions to problems for yourself.'

Question 30 page 101

30 C

After Sonia asks about 'the Spanish 1A module', the tutor explains: 'The module comprises thirty-six hours of class contact, mainly in tutorial groups of sixteen to twenty, and students are expected to do approximately sixty-four hours of private study'.

Questions 25–30: script

RAJAV I'd like to ask a few things about the Applied Chemical Engineering module.

TUTOR Fine. What would you like to know?

RAJAV Well, apart from the work on practical engineering, what other topics are covered?

TUTOR Some that might surprise you. One that students always seem to like includes interviewing techniques, presentation skills and producing written reports.

RAJAV Hmm … they sound interesting. How are they taught?

TUTOR Through lectures, practical classes and personal tutorials. Applied Chemical Engineering lasts all year of course, so there's plenty of time.

RAJAV And what about assessment?

TUTOR Through project work, usually, or dissertation. Not exams as such.

RAJAV Is that the same for the Information Technology part of the module?

TUTOR Yes, things like word processing and learning to create spreadsheets are tested in a similar way on this module.

SONIA That's not the case in some other modules, is it?

TUTOR No, it isn't. Are you thinking of any in particular?

SONIA Yes, I'm considering doing Fluid Mechanics. The work on flow analysis looks interesting and I like the look of some of the other topics, too. So how is that module tested?

TUTOR That's one of those which still uses written exams. The sit-down, formal type I'm afraid!

SONIA Oh that doesn't matter. I quite like that kind as it happens.

TUTOR Pat, you've got a question.

PAT Yes, I was wondering about Science 1 in Chemical Engineering. How is that organized? It's a bit different from other modules isn't it?

TUTOR Yes, it aims to give the necessary basis of physics and biology for those students who haven't studied the relevant subject at A level or equivalent.

In practice it means that students who have already studied physics are excused the physics lectures, while those who've done biology are exempt from attending the biology lectures. In the second part of the module you're assessed on your project work in one of those subjects.

PAT And does the teaching approach differ, too?

TUTOR Yes, particularly in one respect: you are encouraged to learn by working out the solutions to problems for yourself.

PAT I like the sound of that.

TUTOR OK, anything else?

SONIA Yes, I believe it's possible to do a modern language as part of the course. Can you tell me a bit about the Spanish 1A module?

TUTOR Certainly. The main emphasis in 1A is on understanding and speaking, but students also learn to carry out some straightforward reading and writing tasks. Basic aspects of grammar are also introduced and practised. The module comprises thirty-six hours of class contact, mainly in tutorial groups of sixteen to twenty, and students are expected to do approximately sixty-four hours of private study.

SONIA It sounds interesting. I did some Spanish at the Cervantes Institute last year. Passed an exam, in fact.

TUTOR Ah, I'm afraid that means you can't do 1A. The regulations say 'this module may NOT be taken by students with a qualification in Spanish'. Though you could do 1B …

Section 4

Questions 31–33 page 102

31 90,000 / ninety thousand
The prompt for questions 31–33 is 'First, the numbers'. The lecturer talks of 'a rocky meteorite … travelling at around 90 000 kilometres an hour'.

32 4 km / four kilometres
The answer comes in the sentence 'the meteorite vaporized in a ball of fire, carving out a crater about 4 kilometres deep.'

33 40 km / forty kilometres
The answer follows immediately after 32: '… and 40 kilometres in diameter'.

Questions 34–36 page 102

34 C
Although the speaker refers to 'some of the most photogenic impact craters in the world … Acraman is not one of them', which is confirmed by 'half a billion years of erosion has taken its toll. A salt pan surrounded by low hills is all that remains.' A is incorrect: although the lecturer mentions 'a shallow sea', it was '300 kilometres away' at the time of the impact '590 million years ago'. Lake Acraman is referred to later, but this is 'small' and would not contain sea water. B contradicts the correct answer C.

35 A
The key sentences are: 'the true nature of the place dawned on geologist George Williams … in 1979 … gazing at a sheaf of newly acquired satellite images'. B is incorrect since, although his first visit to Acraman was indeed in 1980 ('a year later'), by then he already knew what had happened. Although there is a word from the text ('textbook') in C, it is used as part of the metaphor 'a textbook example of an impact site'.

36 B
Rock from Acraman was also found elsewhere ('the same material turned up at sites 500 kilometres from Acraman'), not just the Flinders ranges 'more than 300 kilometres east of Acraman'. A is incorrect since it implies rock from Acraman was actually found only in the Flinders mountains. C implies the rock was not found in the Flinders.

Questions 31–36: script

LECTURER Lake Acraman in South Australia is Armageddon for the purist. No other meteorite impact on Earth has stamped the surrounding rocks with such an abiding, unequivocal geological record of collision, earthquake, wind, fire and tsunami - the giant waves formed by major earth movements. The story it tells is elemental, without dying dinosaurs or even Bruce Willis to complicate its simple message of destruction. First, the numbers: about 590 million years ago, a rocky meteorite more than 4 kilometres across and travelling at around **90 000** kilometres an hour slammed into an area of red volcanic rock about 430 kilometres northwest of Adelaide. Within seconds the meteorite vaporized in a ball of fire, carving out a crater about **4 kilometres** deep and **40 kilometres** in diameter and spawning earthquakes fierce enough to raise 100-metre-high tsunamis in a shallow sea 300 kilometres away. Ancient, stable and unglaciated, the bedrock of Australia preserves some of the most photogenic impact craters in the world. Acraman is not one of them. Half a billion years of erosion has taken its toll. A salt pan surrounded by low hills is all that remains to mark the site of the cataclysm. The true nature of the place dawned on geologist George Williams of Adelaide University in 1979. Gazing at a sheaf of newly acquired satellite images, he saw the small, circular shape of Lake Acraman surrounded by a ring of faults and low scarps 40 km across, and an outer ring twice this size. A year later he made it to the site. On islands near the centre of the lake, Williams found bedrock shattered in a conical pattern that experts consider a sure sign of a meteorite impact. Except for a crater, which had long since eroded, the area was a textbook example of an impact site. In 1985 further intriguing evidence turned up. Vic Gostin, another Adelaide geologist, had been studying a thin band of fragmented red volcanic rock in 600-million-year-old shale in the Flinders Ranges, more than 300 kilometres east of Acraman. To his bewilderment, the volcanic chunks turned out to be a billion years older than the shale. Where had they come from? Comparing samples, Gostin and Williams found that their rocks were identical: the red rock in the Flinders Ranges had been blasted there from Acraman. Later, the same material turned up at sites 500 km from Acraman.

Questions 37–40 page 102

37 (the) earthquake / shock waves
The speaker talks of 'the *earthquake* ... the shock waves arrived offshore ... stirring up the water ... as the seabed shook.'

38 (the) explosion
The lecturer says 'shattered rock from the *explosion* arrived by air. Pebbles and boulders crashed into the water.'

39 sand
There is a mention of 'a cocktail of silt and *sand*', then 'clouds of silt', and later the speaker says, 'Sand took up to an hour to come to rest, finally bedding down with the silt,' adding 'This mixture would eventually form the next layer.'

40 (the) (huge) waves
The speaker talks of 'layers of increasingly fine sand distorted on top into a wavy, scalloped pattern,' and then explains how they were shaped: '*huge wav*es rolled in, leaving the ripples on the surface that later hardened into rock'.

Questions 37–40: script

LECTURER Everywhere, the bands of fragments showed the same structure: coarse pebbles at the bottom, then a cocktail of silt and sand, then layers of increasingly fine sand distorted on top into a wavy, scalloped pattern. These layers also show, step by step, how the meteorite transformed the floor of an ancient sea hundreds of kilometres away, according to Malcolm Wallace of Melbourne University. First came the **earthquake**. Travelling at about 3 kilometres a second, **shock waves** arrived offshore within a minute or two of the collision, stirring up the water with clouds of silt as the seabed shook. Then shattered rock from the **explosion** arrived by air. Pebbles and boulders crashed into the water, reaching a depth of about 200 metres within a minute. One day they would become the lower band of the Flinders rock. **Sand** took up to an hour to come to rest, finally bedding down with the silt that was also now settling on the sea floor as the effects of the earthquake died away. This mixture would eventually form the next layer. About an hour after the meteorite's impact, **huge waves** rolled in, leaving the ripples on the surface that later hardened into rock. 'Clear as mud' is not an oxymoron. In Acraman, the arid timeless Australian Outback has preserved the closest thing the Earth can boast to a perfect pockmark - the pinnacle of imperfection.

Academic Reading

Passage 1

Questions 1–5   page 105

1   **F**
Referring to the cause, the text mentions 'light's importance in our daily lives', adding 'Light is almost like air.' Describing the effect, it says 'we hardly pay any attention to it,' and 'A human would no more linger over the concept of light than a fish would ponder the notion of water' (lines 18–22).

2   **H**
There is a list of 'exceptions' to the not paying attention to light: 'a rainbow, a sunset,' etc., are the causes; 'certain moments of sudden appreciation' are the effects (lines 23–24).

3   **A**
Lines 62–65 state 'So much of vital importance is communicated by visible light' (the cause) and then 'almost everything from a fly to an octopus has a way to capture it – an eye, eyes, or something similar' (the effect).

4   **D**
The effect 'Black is the way shadows on the moon looked' is given before the cause: 'because the moon has no atmosphere and thus no sky to bounce light into the unlit crannies of the lunar surface' (lines 89–92).

5   **E**
The cause is given in lines 128–131: 'Even though light can be manipulated to go faster than light' ('186,282 miles a second', in the next paragraph), matter can't. Information can't.' The effect is stated: 'There's no possibility of time travel'.

Effects not used

B   Although a 'dark band' is mentioned as occurring between 'rainbows' (line 100), no cause of this is given in the text.

C   The text does refer to 'an Earth-based laser' (line 49) as 'the main power source for long-distance space travel', but this would take place at a 'sizeable fraction of the speed of light', not at over '186,282 miles a second'. It could not be the effect of any other of the causes listed.

G   The fact that they can detect infra-red light is not the effect of any of the causes listed.

Questions 6–10   page 106

6   **Yes**
The writer portrays light as an exception in 'modern physics' by saying 'light won't reduce. Light is light – pure, but not simple', and then: 'No one is quite sure how to describe it. A wave? A particle? Yes, the scientists say. Both.' (line 15).

7   **No**
The writer disagrees with this: 'You can't appreciate the beauty of a rose if you ponder that the colour red is just the brain's interpretation of a specific wavelength of light with crests that are roughly 700 nanometres apart' (lines 34–38)

8   **Not given**
Although there is a mention of the 'moons of Jupiter' and the fact that 'the sun … gives life to our planet' (line 61), the writer does not suggest this is a possibility on other planets.

9   **Yes**
The key sentences are: 'Visible light is … biologically convenient' and 'To see long, stretched-out radio waves, we'd have to have huge eyes like satellite dishes'. The writer's opinion is clear: 'Not worth the trouble!' (lines 71–74)

10   **Yes**
The writer states in lines 93–94 that 'Lynch is a man who, when he looks at a rainbow, spots details that elude most of us.'

Questions 11–13   page 106

11   **a little blue**
Referring to the 'view across the canyon', Lynch is quoted as saying 'the reason those mountains over there look *a little blue* … is because there's sky between here and those mountains' (line 103).

12   **a spaceship**
The *people* are 'science fiction writers and certain overly imaginative folks' who have 'dreamed of' and 'fantasized' that 'you could make a *spaceship* … you could zip around the universe' (line 119).

13   **cesium gas**
The writer states Wang created 'a pulse of light that went faster than the supposed speed limit' and Wang says 'We created an artificial medium

of *cesium gas* in which the speed of a pulse of light exceeds the speed of light' (line 125).

Questions 14–16 page 109

14 True
Surveys by the British AGR are given as evidence that employers 'seek … personal skills and considered these skills more important than specialist knowledge' (lines 36–41). Examples of these skills then follow.

15 False
The sentence beginning 'Clearly, salary differentials …' (line 50) is the first indication that the statement is false. This is later confirmed by 'the average salary paid to an MBA with good work experience is … around two and a half times the average starting salary for a young postgraduate' (lines 62–67).

16 Not given
The four listed questions in lines 82–91 are points for the reader to consider, not statements of fact or of the writer's opinion. The third point, therefore – despite its similarity in meaning to the statement in 16 – is not given, as there is no information that the writer believes this to be *often* the case.

Questions 17–21 page 109

17 C
Quacquarelli is quoted in lines 50–66, referring to 'new graduates with a masters – or even a doctorate'. The words 'In my view' introduce his comment: 'the salary improvement … largely reflects the recruit's age and earning expectancy.'

18 A
Although Hesketh is quoted in the first paragraph, you have to find the second section that quotes him for the answers to both 18 and 21. In paragraph 6, he says 'A postgraduate immediately has an uphill task explaining (to employers) an additional year, or three years, of study' (lines 74–77).

19 B
Blackman's words are introduced by the verb 'explains' in line 20. The rest of this paragraph is summed up by the words in question 19.

20 D
The preposition 'According to' in paragraph 9 introduces Beech's comment 'The MSc … is suitable for students with a good first degree – particularly a non-business first degree – but little or no business experience' (lines 98–102).

21 A
The relevant quote is introduced by 'Anthony Hesketh poses the question whether holding a second degree may even be a disadvantage' (lines 67–69). Question 21 paraphrases his statement
'I have seen many reports over the years suggesting that employers view postgraduates as eminently less employable than those with a first degree' (lines 69–72).

Questions 22–27 page 110

22 job
The summary covers most of the final two paragraphs of the text. Its first sentence paraphrases Maberly: 'Whatever your first degree … a postgraduate business degree can help you gain a competitive edge in an over-crowded *job* market' (line 120).

23 skills
The first part of the sentence corresponds to 'a business masters degree … will enable you to develop *skills* directly relevant to employers' needs' (line 122).

24 motivation
Line 126–128 'Recruiters are highly selective and a vocational qualification is additional evidence of *motivation*,' are paraphrased by the sentence containing question 24.

25 options
Much of the sentence containing option 25 in the summary corresponds to lines 129–130, which include the words 'weigh up the *options*'.

26 company
The sentence 'Try to get sponsorship from a *company*' becomes *preferably with financial assistance from the …* in the summary.

27 future
The last sentence of the summary covers lines 136–137: 'Ultimately the choice is yours – but focus on the *future*, and on your target employer's expectations'.

Questions 28–33   page 111

28 Paragraph B: ix
The records are 'normally constructed in a restricted area' and, in the next paragraph 'local' not from 'a vast area across Europe, northern Eurasia and North America'. Paragraph B also says these records go back 'more than 5000 years', compared with the '600 years' in the Briffa study.

29 Paragraph C: iii
The paragraph says there are 'quite a lot of chronologies available for study' and 'it is possible to compare the records from different areas year by year'. There is then a reference to 'an analysis of 383 modern chronologies, drawn from a vast area', as well as to reading 'the ice record'.

30 Paragraph D: vii
Paragraph D focuses mainly on the process by which volcanoes cause global cooling, which then leads to patterns of thicker and thinner rings in certain trees: 'northern conifers', and more specifically: 'pine'.

31 Paragraph E: vi
The end of D refers to testing 'the findings from the pine density record', followed by 'what European oak was doing across the same…period' in E. The question 'Was oak responding in the same way as the conifers?' is answered in E. There are references to 'this comparison', and oak(s) and conifer(s) are compared.

32 Paragraph F: i
The paragraph begins 'Take the case of 1816' and says what happened then. It later describes events 'in the run-up to 1816', refers to 'the period 1810-20' and 'three unusual elements in less than ten years'. The beginning of G also refers back to the topic of F as: 'the case of 1816' and 'the years just before and after it'.

33 Paragraph G: viii
Paragraph G states 'We can interrogate the trees in areas where there is no historical or instrumental record', making it a *unique record*. There are more references to *other times and places* in the sentence beginning 'Further back in time …'

Headings not used
ii   Paragraph C talks of studying ice layers in Greenland in a similar way to the study of tree rings, not to trees frozen in that ice.
vi   Although paragraph F mentions the 'defeat of Napoleon's invasion', it speculates about whether natural events caused this, not whether it caused climate change.
x   You may expect a paragraph about this, but there isn't one in the text. The writer probably assumes that likely readers already have this knowledge.

Questions 34–36   page 114

34 B
Paragraph A says 'Match the rings from young trees with those from old forest giants', and paragraph B refers to 'overlapping the patterns of wide and narrow rings in successively older timber specimens'.

35 C
'Rafters' (paragraph A) and 'timber' (paragraph B) are both made of wood; both are preceded by 'old' or 'older'. They are also included in the process of making a record: 'Match … and you have a still longer chronology' and 'successfully constructed long tree-ring records by overlapping … '.

36 F
This refers to the 'chronologies' described in paragraph B, which 'date back more than 5,000 years'. 'These records,' it says, are 'normally constructed in a restricted area, using a single species of tree.'

Points not used
A   While dendrochronology can actually provide a complete record of the weather, this is limited to the parts of the world 'south of the tundra' (the cold northern regions) 'and north of the tropics' (the warm area near the Equator).
D   Although ring patterns may overlap, there is no suggestion that the number of rings is the same.
E   This confuses 'chronologies … that date back more than 5000 years' – the result of scientific research – with dendrochronology itself. There is no indication that this is an ancient science.

Questions 37–40 page 114

37 A

Paragraph E states 'the conifers tell only part of the story' within a description of the results of studying the oak, so A is correct. B is incorrect since the phrase 'only part of' means at least some of it must complement that of the oak, while the previous sentence says 'the oaks clearly do respond to the volcanoes in some cases', partly in line with the study of conifers. This also makes C impossible, plus the contrasts between oak and conifer findings in paragraph E. The last sentence of paragraph E does indeed refer to 'global cooling', and the period of study of the oak record was from AD 1400 to the present era, but there is nothing in the text to support option D.

38 A

Paragraph F describes the 'crop failures' and 'unseasonable cold', which in turn was caused by 'the massive eruption of Tambora'. The earthquake mentioned in B happened three or four years before Tambora. C is not supported by evidence: despite the mention of a 'volcanic acid layer' forming in the ice of 'Greenland and Antarctica' following Tambora, there is no evidence that that this led to any melting of the ice caps. D clearly relates to 'the defeat of Napoleon's invasion of Russia': the outcome of a war took place three years before Tambora.

39 B

A exaggerates what the text says: it talks of 'throwing new light on far darker moments in human history' and 'circumstantial evidence that could support some of the stories', not of revealing new historical facts about humanity. B is more limited in scope, suggesting the possibility ('perhaps', 'could') of proving the above, reflecting the references to 'legends'. C is incorrect since, although there is a reference in paragraph G to 'abrupt environmental events', these relate to natural occurrences. D is incorrect since the end of paragraph G focuses on the practical possibility that it might be able to confirm events described in religious texts.

40 D

D uses the word *how* to indicate that the text will focus on ways that the study of tree rings can provide more information about the natural background to human events. A covers only a part of the text which – as the end of paragraph E makes clear – serves mainly to show the potential of dendrochronology. B is based on a misunderstanding of the text, while C overstates its scope.

Sample writing answers

Test 1

Writing Task 1 *page 32*

The linegraph illustrates students who came from Indonesia, Malaysia, Singapore, and Hong Kong in Australia between 1982 and 2000.

The number of students coming from Malaysia in 1982 to in 1993 increased steadily from about 5,000 students to just under 10,000 students whereas that of the other countries increased sharply between about 2,000 students and about 10,000 students. The number of the oversea students in 1993 to in 2000 fluctuate significantly between about 10,000 students and just under 20,000 students with the exception of students coming from Indonesia. There was a dramatically increase in the number of oversea students from Indonesia in 1993 to in 1998, peaking at 26,000 students. There was a slightly drop in the number of students from Indonesia in 1998 to in 2000 from 26,000 students to about 23,000 students.

There was a consirable notice in the number of the oversea students with 5-time increase between 1982 to 2000, except students from Malasia.

Comments

The content of this answer is good, in that it reports the main features of the graph, and also draws particular attention to the significant features. It also attempts to summarize the main message of the graph in the conclusion. Its weakness lies in its lack of cohesion. The writer has strung the sentences together but they do not flow easily from one to the next as there are no linking words. There are some structural and spelling errors, but these do not interfere with communication. The writer has most of the vocabulary he needs to write about graphs. **This answer would probably not achieve Band 7.**

Writing Task 2 *page 34*

In recent years, travelling by plane has become a very common means of transport for many people. Mainly because it's practical, quick and easy, but it also became incredibly cheap and accessible for all. Consequently, people are highly encouraged to choose it and air traffic is increasing rapidly. Although taxing flight tickets more heavily could enable to reduce air traffic considerably, this decision could also lead to many drawbacks.

First of all, if plane tickets become more expensive, many people might reconsider their way of travelling. Therefore, this would certainly encourages more of them to take a train to travel short distances, from a European country to another, for example.

As a result of this, air traffic could decrease and new airport construction not be needed.

On the other hand, to me it is obvious that people will choose to travel using a car or a coach as an alternative way. Therefore, this would lead to lots of noise and pollution on the roads, mostly during holidays. Moreover, economically, the choice of taxing flight tickets heavily could be seen as a discrimination as travelling abroad could only be afforded by wealthy people. Finally, high costs flying might simply diadvantage tourism as it would slow down cultural and economic exchanges between countries.

To sum up, when bearing in mind the consequences of heavy taxes on plane tickets, it does not seem to be an appropriate solution against noise or pollution. Besides, travelling by plane is needed and important to maintain goods exchanges, tourism communication, technology developments ...

Comments

This is an excellent answer in all aspects. There is scarcely a mistake in grammar, despite the use of complex sentences, and it is cogently argued with effective use of link words, displaying a range of logical relationships. The case is argued convincingly with good examples. The text is well planned with a clear introduction, which is not merely a repetition of the question, and a meaningful conclusion. **This answer would probably exceed Band 7**.

Test 2

Writing Task 1 *page 64*

The diagram illustrates the environmental issues by a product over its lifetime.

According to the diagram, first step for the life cycle of a product is product planning and design which is the most significant step for customers as an appearance. Secondly, suppliers have to prepare all of the materials which they need to use for the product. It would appear that most of the people are more likely to concern about the materials that are used during the production because of the quality.

After the process of procurement of the materials is reached, life cycle is followed by production step. As long as a product is ready to sell, initial step carries on with packaging, printing and physical distribution. In addition to this step, there are variety of ways how to make the product more impressive and demanding in the competitive market. That's why, perhaps the most important process is sales, however good quality of materials was used. While suppliers are trying to sell any kind of product, they should persuade customers for either its quality or function as a whole.

In the case of sales, a large proportion of people use varieties of technics how to effect customers in the market even with exaggeration. From customers point of view, they invariably focus on what they need. So, another essential point for suppliers is to meet customer's needs.

Consequently, products are started to be used by customers whether they're satisfied or not. Unless they are satisfied, it's more likely for the product to be given back to the service.

Comments

Although there are some errors in structure, and there might have been more comments on significant stages in the process, this is an adequate answer to the question. The writer displays the ability to use a range of structures and vocabulary. Because the general language is of a high level and flows coherently, it would reach this band level, although comments on the environmental features of the process are lacking. **This answer would probably achieve Band 7**.

Writing Task 2 *page 66*

Nowadays, people are able to reach easily to financial sources by financial instruments such as mortgage loans and credit cards. There are many people who spend money by using credit card or loans without repaying ability. It is the aim of essay to present some benefits and drawbacks when people are not able to borrow easily money.

There are some advantages, when banks don't lend money to people easily. To start with, people are controled their expendition in order not to spend too much money more than their repaying ability. As a result, this is a possible cause that leads to decresing crime in society. Furthermore, when financial institutions have less risks, they can lend money to people with low interest rate. What is more, economy will be safer when financial institutions have no risks. For example, in 1996, the Thai financial institutions lent too much money to people who could not repay. Consequently, it is one of the causes of the crisis in the Thai economy in 1997.

However, when banks are stricter about lending money to people, people need to find another financial source such as to borrow money from mafias or illegal financial institution. As a consequent, this doesn't support economy and danger of their life. Moreover, banks lose the opportunities to earn more money and to increase monitoring cost.

In conclusion, I think every financial instruments are important in economy and encourage economy to be stronger. However, we should be careful of how to use it because it will be a cause of economic problems such as in the crisis of the Thai economy.

Comments

There are many good features in this writing. The question is answered, giving weight to both sides of the argument. There is a clear introduction and conclusion. The writer makes good use of an example from his own experience, and displays appropriate vocabulary for tackling the topic. The ideas are well linked through cohesive devices, and any structural errors are minor. **This answer would probably achieve Band 7.**

Test 3

Writing Task 1 *page 92*

The graphs give information about the number of female students per 100 male students in primary, secondary and tertiary education.

In general, more boys than girls were studying at school both in 1990 and 2000 in all the countries, except in tertiary education in developed countries, and the number of girls per boys was biger in 2000 than in 1990 in the two country groups and in all the educational stages.

Turning to the detail, there were more boys than girls in primary and secondary education. As can be seen, developing countries saw a bigger discrepancy between the numbers of male and female students that developed countries, with the number of girls per 100 boys at 83 in 1990 and 87 in 2000 in primary education. and 72 in 1990 and 82 in 2000 in secondary education. However, in developed countries, the balance of the two was much closer to the ideal, particularly in secondary education, with 98 girls per 100 boys in 1990 and 99 in 2000.

Regarding tertiary education, the balance was even worse than in any other levels of education in developing countries with 66 girls per 100 boys in 1990 and 75 in 2000. On the other hand, in developing countries, the number of girls overtook that of boys at 105 per 100 boys in 1990 and 112 in 2000.

Comments

It is hard to fault this piece of writing. It picks out clearly all the main trends shown in the figures, giving an overall view, and then describing the detail clearly and accurately. The language is sophisticated and complex, using a wide range of vocabulary and structures. It is clearly linked together and is near native speaker in style and use of language. **This answer would probably exceed Band 7.**

Writing Task 2 *page 94*

Recently companies started to use new ways and techniques to compete with others and win the maximum number of clients, one of thoes ways is to recruit talented directors, thoes directors should run the companies and make essential decisions. Therefore, directors receive higher salarys than others, However many spectators believe that directors get more than they deserve.

I would agree that directors of larg companies receive much bigger salarys than other which encreases by time, but I believe that directors deserve these salaries for a number of reasons. Perhaps the most important is the fact that the progress of the company rely on their dicisions, the competition between the companies is vicious and hard, and so, weak establishment cant survive with out good leadership. In addition, diractors work very hard more than some people emagine, they have to study the market, read and analyse every smal detail to make the right dicision. Furthermore, directors are alawys in fear and worriment, they are afraid of giving wrong conclusions and decisions, wich might cause great bereavement to the company and eventually leed to the lose of good position.

However, there are many who disagree with me, arguing that directors receive salaries more than they really deserve. And companies should cut from these salaries and use that money for creating new job opportutunity, improving or building new facilities, take up new equipments, increas the salaries of other workers, or invest this mony in the market.

Comments

The argument here is compelling, although slightly more time is spent on defending the 'for' argument than the 'against'. The writer attempts to use a wider range of vocabulary and structures than is perhaps actually within his competence, but this is a good try. He loses marks for incorrect spelling, and punctuation. There are relatively few structural errors. **This answer would probably not achieve Band 7.**

Test 4

Writing Task 1 *page 115*

The data shows causes which bring people to hospital for teenagers and people of all ages.

The categories can be divided into two groups which are the causes involved with vehicles and the others. The former saw a clear pattern between the genders and ages. Teenagers were more likely to be hospitalized by accidents related to vehicles than adults and more boys than girls were involved in these causes. The most common cause in this group was total transport accidents with 779 cases of boys, 323 of girls, 557 of total teenagers and 305 of total population per 100,000 cases respectively. Pedestrian was the least common casue of hospitalisation in this group with under 50 cases per 100.000 for all the presented age and sex groups.

On the other hand, the distributions in the other causes varied by case. Falls and complications are more common in adults than in teenagers with complications of medicalcare being the most common cause of hospitalisation for the total population among all the causes listed in the table, at 1431 per 100,000 cases. Assault saw the same profile as the causes involved with vehicles. Accidental poisoning was the only cause which more girls than boys were involved in the table.

Comments

The writer has been able to deal only with the significant data, and disregard that which obscures the general trends. He has an excellent command of the language needed to make comparisons, and his points are clearly linked. The wide range of structures is used with almost total accuracy. **This answer would probably exceed Band 7.**

Writing Task 2 *page 116*

Student fees have been a constant subject of debate all round the worlds in recent years. There are many different opinions about this issue and educational systems and financial support to students from states have changed significantly.

In my opinions, there are a number of points that need to be taken into consideration here.

Firstly, the education of students is extremely expensive these day. Students have to pay a great deal of money for various things, such as accommodation, student fees or books. The importance of this is that majority of students can not afford these things. I consider that solutions should be found in financial aid from states to students.

In addition, considering gifted students who do not have money to pay for education. I believe that states should finance their education. For instance, many scientists have recieved money for education in my country. Afterwards, they have discovered and invented a variety of things which have been beneficial for the society. So, states should always support talented students who do not have money. Furthermore, states' financial support can be an extremely motivating and encouragin factor for students. In other words, in terms of leisure and holidays, they can do many things which they cannot do without this states' aid, such as hobbies sport activities or travelling. However, students can use this money in wrong purposes, but generally I claim that this is a good investment for country.

On the other hand, considering the high number of people who want to study, I object strongly that high education should be only provided by states. I claim that states can not pay all extra costs of education for students. As a result, I argue that states and students should reach a compromise regarding this issue.

In conclusion, although there are a number of different points of view regarding costs of university studies, I claim that this should be finance by both students and states. Moreover, states should provide funds which would support gifted students.

Comments

This is generally a good answer in that it is clearly argued, in language which is almost always accurate, although there are a few spelling mistakes and awkward constructions. Cohesive devices are well used. One slight minus point is that the argument is very one-sided, and the writer seems to run out of ideas when he comes to put the opposing argument. Also, he does not display quite the flair and range of vocabulary one might expect at this level. **This answer would probably achieve Band 7.**

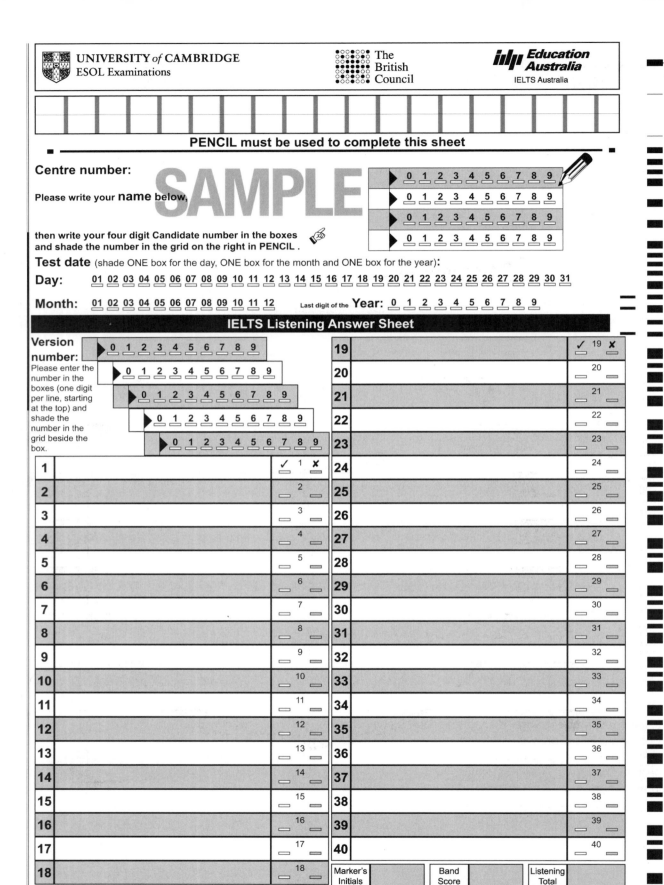

Module taken (shade one box):   Academic ⬚

General Training ⬚

Version number:
Please enter the number in the boxes (one digit per line, starting at the top) and shade the number in the grid beside the box.

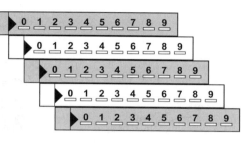

SAMPLE

1		✓ 1 ✗	21		✓ 21 ✗
2		2	22		22
3		3	23		23
4		4	24		24
5		5	25		25
6		6	26		26
7		7	27		27
8		8	28		28
9		9	29		29
10		10	30		30
11		11	31		31
12		12	32		32
13		13	33		33
14		14	34		34
15		15	35		35
16		16	36		36
17		17	37		37
18		18	38		38
19		19	39		39
20		20	40		40

Marker's Initials		Band Score		Reading Total	